This book is due for return on or before the last date shown below.

BASIC TEXTS IN COUNSELLING AND PSYCHOTHERAPY

Series editor: Stephen Frosh

This series introduces readers to the theory and practice of counselling and psychotherapy across a wide range of topic areas. The books appeal to anyone wishing to use counselling and psychotherapeutic skills and are particularly relevant to workers in health, education, social work and related settings. The books are unusual in being rooted in psychodynamic and systemic ideas, yet being written at an accessible, readable and introductory level. Each text offers theoretical background and guidance for practice, with creative use of clinical examples.

Published

Jenny Altschuler
WORKING WITH CHRONIC ILLNESS

Bill Barnes, Sheila Ernst and Keith Hyde
AN INTRODUCTION TO GROUPWORK

Alex Coren
SHORT-TERM PSYCHOTHERAPY

Emilia Dowling and Gill Gorell Barnes
WORKING WITH CHILDREN AND PARENTS THROUGH SEPARATION AND DIVORCE

Gill Gorell Barnes
FAMILY THERAPY IN CHANGING TIMES

Ravi Rana
COUNSELLING STUDENTS

Paul Terry
COUNSELLING THE ELDERLY AND THEIR CARERS

Jan Wiener and Mannie Sher
COUNSELLING AND PSYCHOTHERAPY IN PRIMARY HEALTH CARE

Invitation to authors

The Series Editor welcomes proposals for new books within the Basic Texts in Counselling and Psychotherapy series. These should be sent to Stephen Frosh at the School of Psychology, Birkbeck College, Malet Street, London, WC1E 7HX (e-mail s.frosh@bbk.ac.uk)

Basic Texts in Counselling and Psychotherapy
Series Standing Order ISBN 0–333–69330–2
(outside North America only)

You can receive future titles in this series as they are published by placing a standing order. Please contact your bookseller or, in the case of difficulty, write to us at the address below with your name and address, the title of the series and the ISBN quoted above.

Customer Services Department, Palgrave Ltd
Houndmills, Basingstoke, Hampshire RG21 6XS, England

AN INTRODUCTION TO GROUPWORK

A Group-Analytic Perspective

BILL BARNES, SHEILA ERNST

and

KEITH HYDE

palgrave

Published by
PALGRAVE
Houndmills, Basingstoke, Hampshire RG21 6XS and
175 Fifth Avenue, New York, N.Y. 10010
Companies and representatives throughout the world

PALGRAVE is the new global academic imprint of
St. Martin's Press LLC Scholarly and Reference Division and
Palgrave Publishers Ltd (formerly Macmillan Press Ltd).

ISBN 0–333–63224–9

This book is printed on paper suitable for recycling and made from fully managed and sustained forest sources.

A catalogue record for this book is available from the British Library.

10   9   8   7   6   5   4
08   07   06   05   04   03   02

Editing and origination by
Aardvark Editorial, Mendham, Suffolk

Printed in Great Britain by
Antony Rowe Ltd, Chippenham, Wiltshire

CONTENTS

FOREWORD

Simplicity, complexity and applying the group-analytic approach

Groups are by their nature complex and multifaceted. One of the great merits of this book, as the reader will discover, is that it manages to simplify what is at times an overwhelmingly confusing subject. A group experience can perhaps be divided into three phases. At the start the participants arrive with simple and often stereotyped views: 'This group is going to get me better, my doctor told me so'; 'This staff group is out to psychoanalyse me, no way am I going to let it'; 'That group leader is a cold fish, I certainly can't trust someone who refuses to answer simple questions', or 'We are here to solve our problems, let's get on with it'. There then follows a period in which all seems confusion and uncertainty. How can one possibly make sense of such a profusion of views and feelings and interactions? Far from problems being solved, they seem to multiply. There appears to be no way forward. A silence descends upon the group, or one member talks incessantly. The very existence of the group seems threatened, especially if the following week one or two members fail to turn up.

The group members (and the conductor) have to immerse themselves in this maelstrom and survive. In the end, however, the meaning of the group often emerges in a surprisingly simple way. Someone will make a clarifying remark, or reveal their feelings in an open and honest way, or make a simple suggestion, and the fog suddenly clears and, for the moment at least, all seems to make sense. Participating in such a group experience can be profoundly moving and humbling. It is as though the electricity in the group, often contradictory and dangerous, suddenly earths through one individual who, through a simple remark – 'I feel frightened', or 'Why don't we try it this way?' – moves the feelings and discussion on to a deeper level.

The great innovators in group analysis have mirrored this living experience of groups in their theoretical thinking. Bion's classification into work group, flight or fight, pairing, and dependency is so elegant and simple and yet has a universal applicability which, despite numerous attempts, has yet to be bettered. Another deceptively simple notion is that of Foulkes – of the *setting* and its uses. The regularity of time and place, the arrangement of chairs, the punctuality, the announcement of breaks, the rules of confidentiality, anonymity, and openness – all these form a framework and a boundary, an arena and a space within which emotional life can be played out. The interactions between the individual group member and the setting – lateness or overpunctuality, the wish to contact other members outside the group, where one chooses to sit – are manifestations of the complexity of the individual psyche and its interactions with other psyches within the group. It is the task of the conductor to comprehend these links and to communicate them in a simple way to the group.

This dialectic is nowhere more evident than in a large organisation such as a hospital or mental health unit. I believe that group analysis has an invaluable part to play in the running of such an organisation. Units like these usually run on simple hierarchical principles – lines of responsibility, converging eventually on a leader such as chief executive or clinical director. In the UK successive waves of government policies have shaped the way in which these organisations function: supervision registers, the care programme approach, primary nursing, risk management. Organisational anxiety is handled in the classic Menzies-Lyth (1959) fashion (see Chapter 8). A complex bureaucratic structure is created to give the appearance that something is being done. This is not to say that some of these innovations cannot be useful in systematising thought and avoiding lackadaisical or risky work practices. But from a group-analytic perspective, of which this book is such a fine exposition, they avoid two main issues. First, this 'paperwork' gives the impression that, if procedures are rigorously followed, all will be well. Mental pain, disaster, death, loss, disability, mistakes and perversion will somehow be miraculously swept aside, only to recur if procedures have been incorrectly pursued. Second, paperwork becomes a substitute for the mental work of the group – the work of containing fears and anxieties on a collective basis, of facing inadequacy, the partial successes which are often the best that can be hoped for, the inevitable relapses and failures.

There is indeed an irony in this: the more the group is able to face its weaknesses, the stronger it becomes; the more it can admit to fears and failures, the less likely failure is to occur. This may seem an unsubstantiated claim, but there is good evidence that running a staff group on an acute admission ward in itself reduces the incidence of untoward 'incidents' so feared by management. The *mechanism* by which this happens needs further research – is it more open communication between staff members, clarification of lines of responsibility and leadership, greater security for patients in knowing that the staff support each other and so are more able to hold projections?

A staff group on an admissions ward or community mental health team can be a fragile thing. Workers are often suspicious, or contemptuous: 'They are in there for hours on end contemplating their navels, while we out here are doing the real work.' The management may view such groups as subversive, ambivalently damning the group with faint praise, or asking for endless evaluation sheets to be filled in by all participants before they can let it go ahead. Such groups can be divisive, however much their overt aim is the opposite – the ward can be split into 'groupies' and those who refuse to participate. Membership can fluctuate wildly. Talking in groups can become a substitute for clear treatment plans and decisive leadership. The simple can get bogged down in the complex. The value of such a group will emerge slowly over time, and may not be apparent to those looking for instant results. Anyone planning to set up such a group will do well to read a book such as this which emphasises the need for careful planning, forming an alliance with key figures in an organisation, and being sensitive to the inevitable threat that a small pocket of space in which anxiety can be exposed and held will create in an organisation dedicated to its suppression. It is all too easy to blame 'them' – the management, the insensitive ward manager, the suspicious consultant psychiatrist – so losing hold of the basic group-analytic principle that negative aspects of group phenomena will often be carried by one or two individuals, and disowned by the group as a whole.

A similar process of projection applies to psychiatry itself, especially in a general hospital setting, which within medical culture is often seen as the repository for all that is uncomfortable, awkward, untreatable and emotional – the psychic equivalent of the clinical waste department where difficult feelings can be located so that the rest of the hospital can run with its accustomed smooth sterility. The main function of acute psychiatric wards is containment of threats of disturbance or violence to self or others. One might cynically suggest that that, ultimately, is why governments fund psychiatric services at all. Through early intervention and 'assertive outreach' many patients who previously would have been admitted to such wards are now contained in the community by teams of intensive carers, working in the patients' home. There is much debate in psychiatric circles about how many in-patients beds are needed, although all admit that there is a residuum without which psychiatric services cannot function effectively over long periods. How do such services 'work'? Partially of course it is the new anti-psychotic and anti-depressant medications. Partially it is the specific psychological interventions such as reduction in family anxiety or helping psychotic patients to live with their delusions. But perhaps more important than both of these is the strength of the group in reducing anxiety and helping the sufferer to feel held and supported. Research has shown that psychological distress reduces following hospital admission long before the drugs have had time to take effect. A vital task of the organisation is to harness the containing power of groups. This applies both in in-patient settings and in the community, where mental health workers can only function effectively if they are true teams, working together to a common task, supporting each other, exploring and reconciling differences when they arise.

It is all too easy to see only the instrumental aspects of such work – the tasks of delivering 'packages' of care, and to miss the matrix out of which these arise, and which, if malfunctioning, can undermine the whole enterprise. Many ward staff offer their patients counselling or group therapy sessions, and these can certainly be valuable. But if the overall milieu of the ward is dysfunctional – if staff do not communicate, if there is splitting, if leadership shirks its tasks – then all is undermined. A ward or community team is like a family, and the principles of healthy family function can be applied to it. There needs to be a clear leadership structure, with good communication and mutual respect between men and women. The clients/patients, like children in a family, need to know where they are and where the boundaries lie. At the same time there needs to be a warm atmosphere of open communication, acceptance, and a culture of humour and fun. A psychologically dysfunctional ward, like a surgical ward infested with multiple drug-resistant bacteria, may begin to cause the very disturbances it purports to cure. Dependency becomes rife, patients learn to express distress via cutting and overdosing rather than through open communication, an 'adolescent' feel to the culture begins to build up in which staff are seen as dictatorial and neglectful, the patients impossible and 'bad'. The idea of psychiatric illness gets lost and a culture of 'blaming the victim' develops. In these conditions of 'malignant alienation' suicides are most likely to occur. Written protocols may help to some extent in 'risk management', but if the ward atmosphere is wrong, and there is no systematised group forum such as a staff support group where difficult issues can be discussed openly, the likelihood that mistakes will happen is greatly increased.

In my view the use of group-analytic principles in staff support in psychiatric settings, and where possible median groups for patients and staff together, is an essential counterpoise to balance the emphasis on focused interventions and protocols that are currently so fashionable. There is a danger that the skills needed to run – or even to participate in – such groups will atrophy under a welter of regulatory paperwork. These skills are not simply those of 'interpersonal technology' or 'psychosocial interventions', but a mature capacity to reflect on oneself in relation to others – the ability to understand and work with transference and countertransference. This timely book is a significant contribution to the growing recognition of the importance of psychotherapy in all its forms as part of a modern psychiatric service. A basic principle of psychotherapy is the importance of relationships as fundamental to human health. The individual in relationship to groups – the family, work groups and the wider society – is the province of group analysis. The social nature of man is a simple truth, whose complex implications are explored with almost deceptive clarity throughout this volume.

JEREMY HOLMES, MD
MRCP, FRCPsych

Consultant Psychotherapist,
North Devon and
Chair of the Psychotherapy Faculty,
Royal College of Psychiatrists

ACKNOWLEDGEMENTS

This book is dedicated to Bill Barnes who died, prematurely, before its publication. Bill represented an important element in our project because, like many of our prospective readers, he was not a group analyst. He was a very experienced group clinician, a knowledgeable theoretician and teacher who used a group-analytic understanding in his clinical practice, in supervision and as the clinical director of a consultation and psychotherapy service. He encompassed a complex approach to psychotherapy which we hope this book will encourage in its readers.

Completing the work the three of us had started together, as staff members of the Manchester Course in Group Psychotherapy, in the shadow of Bill's illness and untimely death was a painful experience.

We hope that this book reflects the tradition of the Institute of Group Analysis which over the past twenty-five years has offered courses to thousands of students who work in groups using diverse approaches, but have found that group-analytic thinking had something special to offer them in their understanding of groups.

We would like to thank the many students who over the years have attended the Manchester Course in Group Therapy and in particular those group members who agreed to the publication of their group. Without these students the book could not have been written. We were delighted to be asked by Stephen Frosh to contribute to the series and have appreciated his patience and encouragement, despite his misgivings about the group writing of a book on groups.

SHEILA ERNST AND KEITH HYDE

Every effort has been made to trace all the copyright holders but if any have been inadvertently overlooked the publishers will be pleased to make the necessary arrangements at the first opportunity.

INTRODUCTION

Looking at groups: what is a group-analytic approach?

We all have a great deal of experience of being in groups and observing them in everyday life. Our interest lies in helping people to make fuller use of these observations and experiences to enhance their participation as group therapists, in groups they work in or belong to for social purposes. Those who want to become more effective in groups enrol on groupwork training courses and read books like this hoping to learn something which will enable them to make sense of the jumble of experiences which constitute participation in a group. They want to utilise the great potential of people being together in a group to ensure that it is fulfilled and the outcome is not destructive.

In the first seminar of the Groupwork Course, which inspired us to write this book, we asked new students to share their own experiences of groups. We chose not to start by telling them about the group-analytic approach and its history. This simple decision reflects an underlying approach to our work in groups which we hope this book will convey. The reader or student is encouraged to be aware of what she already knows; to heighten her awareness of what she observes and to contextualise her observation.

This seminar represents a microcosm of views and a variety of models or ways of thinking emerge. Abercrombie, a pioneer of using group methods in teaching, wrote: 'During the discussion the students were mutually testing and modifying their schemata, and as a result of reorganising their store of experience in this way were able later to make more valid interpretations' (1989). She helped medical students to develop their capacity to formulate scientific judgements, while we use group methods to formulate our understanding of how groups themselves work. Abercrombie's idea that through group interaction participants can be helped to mutually test and modify their internal schemata (the observer's basic reactions, expectations, assumptions and attitudes) constitutes the **group-analytic** approach to the group as a therapeutic and an educational setting. Our book considers this approach and how to use it in groups. As one student on our course put it:

I came on the course with experience of co-conducting therapy groups and working in community groups but I could only think about individual group members or how I felt in the group. I realised I was being offered a new language or a new pair of glasses which helped me to hear or see my perceptions of individuals and my own feelings, in terms of what had been happening in the group. I began to have a way of thinking about how I could behave in a group.

Defining a Group

What is it that turns a collection of people into a group? If we look at pictures of a number of people together how can we tell whether they constitute a group?

A picture of swimmers in the sea shows a number of people involved in a similar activity but it is only when some of the swimmers start to play ball together that we can see they form a distinct group. A group is more than people who happen to be doing the same thing at the same time in the same place; to be a group, the people must have some connection, some way in which they come together (either literally or in their minds) with a common aim, purpose or function. This defines the boundaries of the group, separating it from the surrounding environment of which nevertheless it is a part. There is a **boundary** around the swimmers who play a game together, separating them from other swimmers.

Now there is a relationship between group members, defining the group itself and being defined by others as separate from the surroundings and its environment, which implies the potential for tension within several systems. The swimmers playing with the ball have a sense of their game and their group which partly derives from there being others who are not part of the game. They may find that others try to join in their game or try to take the ball away. How the group of swimmers responds to such interactions is important: to continue the group activity they need to maintain a boundary, yet people from the wider environment can support that continuation or attempt to close it down.

This simple example raises some basic questions about groups. What holds them together? What causes them to fragment? How do they relate to their environment? The **cohesion** of the swimmers' group may be increased by the fear of attack on their boundaries. They may submerge their internal differences in order to keep others out. Group cohesion needs some sense of differentiation or opposition from others to keep it going. Sometimes the nature of the attack or the group constitution means that it cannot become more cohesive, and the group fragments. Chapter 7 looks at the effects of environmental factors on the group.

The boundary also creates tension within the group leading to fruitful interaction in which group members are able to modify themselves and their views in the light of what they see and hear; it may also lead to destructive interaction, irresolvable conflict and fragmentation. Will the swimmers be able to sort out their differences of opinion about the rules of their game, the number of passes that a particular person gets or one player's irritation at another one's showing off? Chapter 4 shows a group gradually developing cohesion and resilience despite setbacks and Chapters 3, 5 and 6 look at how this development can be facilitated.

This book addresses the complex reasons for these many different potential outcomes within a group, looking at the interconnections between past and present, conscious and unconscious, individual and group, inside and outside; thinking about how we can structure a group and develop our interactions within the group to enable the group to use its tensions creatively. To make the book more accessible we include a summary of **learning points** at the end of each section.

LEARNING POINTS

- A collection of people becomes a group when those people come together with a common aim. This aim differentiates group from not-group, and **boundaries** are drawn.
- The group needs this differentiation from others to develop **cohesion**, but boundaries bring with them the potential for internal and external tension and conflict.

Observation as the Starting Point

Being in a group constitutes a learning process in itself. Learning about group therapy cannot be done either through teaching **groupwork skills** or adopting a theoretical understanding which is then applied to any group. We encourage careful observation of what is happening in the group and concur with the psychoanalyst Enid Balint who wrote: 'The best thing an analyst can do to begin with is just to make observations and not be too worried if he cannot fit them into any particular theory' (1993).

Observation cannot be an entirely neutral activity as Abercrombie points out: 'Our reaction to the present bombardment of information involves ignoring some of it' (Abercrombie, 1989) and she looks at how we decide what is relevant. We can develop an awareness of how we choose to notice some things and can distinguish observation (albeit subjective) from making inferences about a client/patient or about a group. Balint distinguishes between what she observes the patient to be doing (for instance making a polite remark) and the analyst's inference from this observation (that the patient is trying to please the analyst). This can be applied to groups. In the book excerpts and observations from groups are distinguished from inferences and commentary.

Observing what happens in a group draws on two traditions of observational study. One is the mother–baby observation which is part of many individual psychoanalytically orientated trainings and the other is participant observation used in social anthropology.

In mother–baby observation the observer records what she sees and her own emotional response to the situation so that both can be discussed. This provides an illuminating opportunity to distinguish between what is noticed, what effect this might have had on the observer for her own personal reasons and what she might have been picking up unconsciously about the mother–baby interaction.

After observing a mother and baby, where the mother talked about her difficulties in getting time for herself, complained about her dad being too soft on the baby and stopped her husband from attending to the baby, the observer felt exhausted. In discussing the material she realised that her exhaustion might be linked to finding it difficult to bear 'Michael's [the baby's] vulnerability being exploited or ignored at times, and to see the degree of the mother's upset' (Miller et al., 1989). The observer learned that her own feelings could both impair her vision of the interaction between mother and baby and be used as an indicator of what was happening in that relationship. This link between observation and feeling is an important part of the training of any counsellor or groupworker; understanding your own responses can help you to hear what is going on.

Group-analytically trained sociologists have added another dimension to participant observation which is the use of the observer's **free association** and **countertransference**. In a participant observation study of the spread of Protestant churches in Ecuador, Rohr (1993) explored the appeal of these new churches to the population, other than any material advantages they offered. Through noting what came into her mind as she observed the service, and the details of what she could see, hear and smell, she was led to memories of her own childhood and the part that her first visit to church had played in her learning to gain pleasure from controlling her body. She sat through a service desperately needing to go to the lavatory but consoling herself because she was being 'a big girl'. She used her countertransference to enrich her understanding of the observations, hypothesising that a similar process of pleasure in self-control might be taking place for the Ecuadorians.

Observation encourages paying close attention to what you actually see and take in with your senses in a group and then registering your own emotional response to the group setting, recognising that it will not be *objective*. A further sifting takes place, distinguishing your own personal issues from indicators of the emotional tone and interaction in the group.

LEARNING POINTS

■ Observation is the best starting point for understanding what happens in a group. We consider the traditions of mother–baby observation from psychoanalysis and participant observation from sociology.
■ Both traditions encourage receptivity to the observer's own thoughts (**free association**) and feelings (**countertransference**), however apparently strange or illogical.
■ Having given free rein to thoughts and feelings, personal responses to the group can be distinguished from those evoked by the group.

A Way of Classifying Groups

Groups are so versatile as a medium for helping people that we need some way of codifying how we use them. Whitaker[1] suggests that it is useful to think about a three-dimensional grid in which we connect the *type of patient* (or *group member*), with the *purpose of the group* and the *type of group*. This can help us to think about why (for what *purpose*) we would choose to establish a particular *type of group* for a particular kind of potential *group member*. The future groupworker is asking herself three questions: Whom do you want to help? What do you hope to achieve? How can the group be set up to do this? These issues are discussed more fully in Chapter 3.

---

1. 'This is taken from written notes prepared by Dorothy Stock Whitaker for a presentation on "The Versatility of Group as a Medium for Helping People"' at a Day Workshop held in Liverpool on 18th October 1996, made available to the authors and used by them with Dorothy Stock Whitaker's permission.

The list below illustrates the wide range of groups we find when we asked several groupworkers to tell us about the groups they are curently conducting.

- An ante-natal group
- a social skills group in a day centre
- an out-patient analytic group
- a drop-in group
- a group for people who hear voices
- a group about appropriate sexual behaviour for people with learning difficulties
- a staff group at a residential children's home
- a group for sex offenders
- a psychodrama group
- a reminiscence group for elderly people
- a dietician's group
- a therapy group in a resource centre for people from ethnic minorities
- an anxiety management group
- an open group for drug users
- an experiential group for students
- a group for people who harm themselves
- a bereavement group
- a discussion group for people with long-standing mental health problems.

What happens if we try to map some of these groups using Whitaker's three dimensions?

An ante-natal group

Whom do you want to help? (type of group member)
This is a group for prospective parents. They will not necessarily be people who have had particular physical or emotional difficulties but are brought together because they are sharing an experience of a life transition; that of becoming parents.

What can be achieved? (purpose of the group)
Bringing together a group of people who are shortly to become parents can have several purposes, practical, emotional and social. The group may help them to develop practical skills both in preparation for the birth of the baby and in caring for the baby. It may also be a place where prospective parents can share their hopes and fears about the anticipated change in their lives. This in turn might lead to some reworking of their

own childhood experiences as part of the preparation for parenthood. The group also provides a social forum where prospective parents can meet others and develop relationships which may be very important in combatting the isolation of becoming a parent and the inevitable consequent changes in lifestyle.

How can the group be set up to do this? (type of group)
The first constraint on an ante-natal group is that it needs to be structured so as to encompass members who will attend at a relevant point during the woman's pregnancy. The group will need to be able to encompass a certain level of uncertainty so that members may suddenly not attend because the mother has gone into labour. In fact the uncertainty in the group reflects the uncertainty which is part of this life transition. The group may want to expand its boundary to include a visit after the baby's birth by the parent(s) and baby. The group conductor will have to decide how much time she wants for structured exercises and didactic teaching and how much for free discussion, depending on the balance she wants to achieve between practical learning, emotional sharing and encouraging future social contacts. She will probably choose to have a group which has a specific and limited membership and a time limited life. She will have to make other crucial decisions based on the aims of the group such as the length of each group meeting and the number of meetings.

Let us compare this to an **out-patient analytic group** asking the same three questions.

Whom do you want to help? (type of group member)
Anyone who is experiencing emotional or psychological difficulties but who can still function in the everyday life well enought to live in the community and tolerate the anxieties inherent in attending therapy. The prospective group member often sees his problems lying in his relationships with other people. A life crisis may precipitate his seeking therapy but he can recognise that the source of his problems may be in his earlier life. People of all ages, either sex, at any particular life stage and from varied social and ethnic backgrounds might be helped by this type of group.

What can be achieved? (purpose of the group)
The group should enable people to be more open in personal relationships and to find the previously hidden qualities which allow them to achieve their potential.

How can the group be set up to do this? (type of group)

Here the group will need to provide as much safety as possible for the group members so that through exploring their relationships with each other in the group they can come to understand what happens between them which is so damaging and restricting in their daily lives. For the group to be a place in which this kind of exploration and even experimentation can take place it is important that it is clearly separated from the group members' daily lives. The group members do not form a social network outside the group sessions nor does the group have any practical tasks. It needs to develop into a place in which emotional exploration can take place. The group needs to be able to allow group members to stay in the group for long enough for such deep exploration and changes to take place.

A **drop-in group**, in contrast, poses difficulties in creating a group with an uncommitted membership.

Whom do you want to help? (type of group member)

People who want social contact, emotional support, advice, help or have some undefined need. Their ability to maintain consistent personal relationships varies. They may lead chronically chaotic lives, may lack ordinary living skills and their capacity to access and use resources to overcome problems is impaired either by serious mental illness or persistent difficulties in interpersonal functioning. Alternatively, a drop-in group may be for people who have functioned adequately but are suddenly at a point of crisis either because of external circumstances (for example refugees) or because of internal conflicts (for example over their sexual orientation). A drop-in may be part of a larger programme of care.

What do you hope to achieve? (purpose of the group)

To enable those attending to continue functioning at their present level, cope with their immediate crisis, maintain contact and continue to comply with agreed care plans and treatment. To reduce isolation through group members slowly developing an attachment to the group, gaining support from and learning to offer help and advice to each other. Developing relevant practical skills.

How can the group be set up to do this? (type of group)

The group will be very long term, yet each session has a different membership and must be treated as a separate group. The structure must aim to address each member's needs while being reliable and consistent. Shared leadership will be necessary to provide continuous cover. Directive leadership is necessary to draw in the strangers and help members to relate to each other. There may be structured discussion or activities. Attachment to the group may occur if the last session was helpful.

Already we can see that using this mapping device has implications for how we think about our groups. It could usefully be applied to any of the groups on this list or any others with which the reader may be familiar. Many of these groups will have been started by group leaders who have a sense of the therapeutic value of groups without being familiar with group-specific phenomena or a theory which helps them to understand what happens in groups. The therapists competent in cognitive work with individuals can use a new pair of glasses to understand the group aspects of their therapy, particularly when things start *not going according to plan*. We will look at this later, along with another example from the list (the staff group at a residential children's home) with observation as the starting point.

LEARNING POINTS

- There are many ways in which groups can be used to help people. They can be mapped onto three dimensions: type of group member, purpose and type of group.
- The starting point is always a person or persons – the potential group membership: Whom do you want to help? What can be achieved? How can the group be set up to do this?

What a Group-analytic Approach Means

The group-analytic approach is helpful in understanding our work in both analytic and all the other groups in our earlier list. We do not have the expertise, for instance, of skilled cognitive therapists running a structured support group for agoraphobics, neither do we suggest that they should turn their support group into an analytic group instead. Group analysis offers a way of thinking about the group phenomena that bubble away under the structures that groupworkers design to help individuals within a group setting. It is also concerned with what happens when there is *no* fixed structure (of discussion or activities) or set agenda. Insights from this laboratory of group analysis can be applied in all group settings.

In Chapter 2 we show how group analysis is based in psychoanalytic thinking but goes beyond applying individual psychoanalysis in a group setting to looking at how the group-specific phenomena mould the dynamics within groups. We use Foulkes' term **group conductor** throughout the book to refer to the group therapist, leader or facilitator since it reflects the way in which her practice is integrated with her theoretical approach; her free-floating attention alights now on the individual(s) and now on the group but the *individual* does not get lost as can seem to happen in approaches that focus solely on the group as a whole. Integrating the individual and group perspectives we offer therapy *in* the group, *of* the group and *by* the group as opposed to people taking turns in having individual therapy with an audience.

Group analysis combines the deep insight into personality derived from psychoanalysis with insights into relationships between people drawn from social psychology. However, for Foulkes (its originator), the individual and the social are abstractions. What the conductor has before her is the group, which is an ever-changing pattern of figure ground relationships – a holistic concept drived from Gestalt psychology. Group analysis is itself an integration of a number of approaches formerly isolated from one another. It is open to developments in the theories of individual and group psychology.

In the following chapters we view human relationships both in terms of transference and projection, and of their ordinariness. We demostrate our close attention to transactions within the charmed circle of the group boundary and an appreciation of the wider social context of the world outside. The model is systemic and sees the group system as within other systems. Again the key is integration, as the conductor integrates her observations and her feelings in her practice. Few of the groups listedearlier were run along group-analytic lines, but the group-analytic synthesis of psychoanalytic, sociological, holistic and systemic theory and practice can illuminate them all and, when they are stuck, it can get them going again.

Understanding What Happens in Groups

The attitude or mind-set of the observer is to glean information about what is going on in groups through looking at the external data (what you actually perceive through your senses) and the internal data provided by your own responses. Chapter 4 is pivotal, describing the life of a group and the observations and inferences of its conductor.

Chapter 2 shows someone joining a group (which is everyone's starting point with groups) and looks at how individual psychodynamic practice and theory relate to the group experience. It also introduces some specifically group-analytic terms and concepts. Starting a group and building a group-analytic approach into the most practical details is the subject of Chapter 3. The following three chapters show how a group develops through certain recognisable stages, and the role played by the conductor in facilitating group processes. Chapters 7 and 8 look at the impact of social issues on groups and applying a group-analytic perspective to a work context. The book ends with a discussion of how readers may develop their work with groups, whether as a specialism or as one part of their generic work.

A New Pair of Glasses

These two examples enlarge on how group-analytic thinking offers a new perspective for viewing groups.

In a group for people who are trying to overcome their agoraphobic symptoms, the therapists find that their plans are apparently disrupted by one member. How can group-analytic thinking help?

The group aims to use the shared experience of agoraphobia to create a supportive environment enabling members to work in a behavioural way on their problems.

CASE EXAMPLE

The therapy group meets weekly for eight weeks. One of the two male group members becomes increasingly angry; time is spent on trying to calm him instead of proceeding with the plan for each meeting. The co-therapists are desperate. They set homework, try to have feedback sessions but their plan is constantly disrupted. The rebellious man attends while other members are discouraged, turn up late or don't do their homework. No one complains about the man's disruption although some members moan about other people in their lives who annoy them.

The therapists' own cognitive-behavioural training had equipped them to understand and work with faulty thinking and self-defeating behaviours, but without much emphasis on their developmental or interpersonal aspects. They wanted to modify their structures and offer the troublemaker some individual therapy, focused on anger management, to prepare him for the next group. Group-analytic thinking means asking: 'What does this man's behaviour and the group's response say both about him as an individual and about the whole group?'

The problem becomes part of the group's own process: what are the underlying reasons for people's fear of leaving their homes; being agoraphobic? Perhaps there is a need to control feelings and thoughts which could seem dangerous, expressed by avoiding external dangers outside home. Beginning to challenge their agoraphobia (by attempting behaviour modification) may arouse these hidden feelings. This man may be expressing anger *on behalf* of the other group members. Their lateness, not complaining and not doing the homework could be passive ways of joining in with his anger. Perhaps the group is trying to resolve its conflicts, about whether or not to overcome their debilitating symptom, by generating a potential fight between the *problem* man and his therapists. In family terms, he might represent the angry adolescent inside each group participant who never worked out the family conflicts that enable the adolescent to take his or her place in the world.

Understanding what is happening can be interesting and a relief for the therapists, helping them to maintain their work in the group. However, this is not an analytic group (of the type we will look at in subsequent chapters) so the therapists may decide to use their insight within the existing group structure. They may suggest that each group member thinks about what would make them as angry as the *angry* member, implying that they are all angry and offering a safe way of expressing it. Alternatively they may include a report on each person's feelings while doing the homework allowing for difficulties to be shared. They might initiate a time for talking about group issues such as people turning up late and not doing their homework, suggesting through the structure that this behaviour is part of the group's business rather than being *naughty.*

The second group is a staff group for residential social workers from a children's home and is conducted by a psychologist. The members suggested that he chatted with them over coffee for a while and then walked over with them to start the session in a more companionable and relaxed atmosphere. The psychologist declined, keeping to his nine o'clock start, sensing this was the right thing to do but without quite knowing why. He felt he was being controlling and unsympathetic in sticking to the time boundaries of the session. He felt for the residential workers, stuck between uncaring rigid management and uncared-for wayward youngsters.

CASE EXAMPLE

> No one turns up for the first two sessions at the training centre until about twenty-past nine, apart from the psychologist... When they arrive they talk about being badly treated by their managers at head office, who want everything done by the book these days. Management is controlling and unappreciative of their efforts to provide sympathetic care for very disturbed (and disturbing) young people. There was some disagreement in the group about the relative merits of discipline and nurture (most being for the latter) in their work, but total agreement about being a low pay, low status group struggling to provide a decent service. When asked about turning up late, they said that they always have a coffee in the canteen on training days.

Seeing himself as a participant observer attending to the group process could help the psychologist to understand his discomfort at sticking to his job as facilitator, which includes managing time boundaries. Maybe it was a gut reaction (countertransference) to being seen, and feeling treated, as if he were the uncaring and unsympathetic management. Perhaps the staff were acting like their wayward young residents. He felt tempted to leave his structure and join them in the canteen just as they valued caring relationships more than structures, rules and regulations. He had observed that they spoke more about how neglected they were than about the young people whose neglect had brought them into their care. He began to see that their job was very difficult and wondered what had attracted them to it. They were expected to set boundaries for children who kept breaking them and to provide them with the care that most of them had never had before.

This is a complex situation in which the daily interactions between the staff and children are affected by background factors. Society has unrealistic expectations of what can be achieved in residential homes for very little money and this puts pressure on the staff. National policies impose financial and other constraints which management must implement. The staff then experience management as controlling and unsympathetic and do not feel supported in their difficult work. Some of the staff may also be trying to come to terms with their own childhood, hoping to offer something better than they had themselves.

Inviting the psychologist to join them in the canteen for coffee (instead of meeting for their group session) was the staff's way of showing him what happens to them in their daily work with the children. The staff are constantly invited or challenged to collude in breaking boundaries. Implicitly the staff are saying to the psychologist: 'The way for us to like you as a supportive authority figure is for you to agree to break the rules with us.' The psychologist hypothesises that this is the message the children give to the staff and he can see how difficult it is for them to be good authority figures or parents. They do not know how to combine being safe, reliable and laying down the law, when necessary, with providing love and care to very challenging young people. Instead, the staff may deal with these two conflicting aspects of their work by seeing themselves as providing decent care and projecting the unpopular control aspect onto the management. In the group session they avoided their own dilemmas about combining nurturing and authority by only mentioning authority in connection with their managers' authority over them.

The psychologist used his observations of the staff group and his reactions to them as indicators of the way that they might be feeling. He was tempted to abandon his authority but did not because he felt uneasy about doing so. Respecting his observations and feelings, in the way we are suggesting, might have given him confidence through understanding his decision. To have blurred the boundaries would have robbed the staff of the opportunity to talk about the dilemmas of working with these young people. Just like the young people, the staff support group requires *both* boundaries *and* talk.

We have noted the importance of:

1. careful observation of the group
2. registering one's own feelings
3. sifting out which aspects of one's overall response reflect personal issues and which might be to do with the feel of the group itself.

This means that the conductor is somehow expected to be both *objective* and *subjective* – how is this possible? We tend to think of objectivity and subjectivity as poles apart, one the domain of statisticians and scientists and the other of poets and mystics. The therapists in the first example were desperate, but pulled away from their subjective response to their situation into an objective approach not to the group but to the individual. In the second example, the psychologist feared losing his objective grasp of the situation and drowning in the subjective feel of the group. It is as if you can be only one thing or the other, objective or subjective:

> The businessman who assumes that this life is everything and the mystic who asserts that it is nothing, fail, on this side and on that, to hit the truth. 'Yes, I see, dear; it's about halfway between', Aunt Juley had hazarded in earlier years. No; truth, being alive, was not halfway between anything. It was only to be found by continuous excursions into either realm, and although proportion is the final secret, to espouse it at the outset is to ensure sterility. (Forster, 1956)

LEARNING POINTS

- Your own thoughts and feelings are very valuable data and you need to let them into your field of observation so that you can use them and think about them.
- Your field of observation is framed by the type of group and its purpose (the group's task), which link closely with the role of the conductor (your task). You need to be clear about your role and then stay in it.
- **Group analysis** offers a way of making sense of these data and using them to further the aims of the group.

2

THE INDIVIDUAL AND
THE GROUP

Group therapy from the individual's point of view: how can it help me, or my client/patient?

Introduction

Georgina has felt low recently, nothing cheers her up and she consults her GP. She forgets things and is not her normal efficient self at home or at work. She is 35 but fears that her apparently failing memory may be a sign of pre-senile dementia. The doctor asks various medical questions and arranges for tests to rule out possible organic causes; he also asks about herself and her circumstances and discovers that her father died recently after a prolonged period as an invalid. She had not visited him and cared for him as much as she had wanted, because of the other demands on her; she also found her step-mother difficult.

The tests prove negative and the GP, thinking that the problems may be emotional, refers her to the practice counsellor. After some exploratory sessions the counsellor suggests that Georgina might find it useful to talk about her problems with others who are also in difficulty. She is referred to the out-patients' department of her local hospital with a view to her joining a group-analytic group. Georgina has faith in her doctor and the counsellor and is relieved that other people have similar difficulties so she agrees to try, although she is unsure how a group can help her. She wonders if it would be better to talk to an *expert* about her personal problems.

The reader, or her client/patient may, like Georgina, have an intuitive sense that a group of people can help each other, or have had the experience of being helped or helping others in a group setting. To understand *how* group therapy works, or to ensure that therapy groups will be therapeutic for the individual members, there needs to be an underlying theory which both accounts for people's unhappiness or symptoms (which common sense cannot explain) and understands how being with other people in a therapeutic setting can address them.

There are many ways of understanding psychological symptoms: for the cognitive psychologist Georgina's thoughts interfere with her feelings, while the interpersonal therapist or counsellor concentrates on the disturbance her symptoms cause in her current communication with others. Our own experience has drawn us to a psychoanalytic model of personal development which sees the roots of an individual's psychological problems in the earliest relationships with others and how these manifest themselves in current relationships in daily life and in a therapeutic setting. The group-analytic framework goes beyond the formative impact of early relationships within the family (in its broadest definition) to point out that these are affected by the social and physical environment (context) within which the family lives.

Foulkes brought both of these perspectives to the therapeutic work he developed with groups. He drew on his knowledge and experience as a psychoanalyst and his belief that social and environmental issues were to be found at the core of individual personal development (see Dalal, 1998). This meant that the group-analytic approach was different from individual analysis/psychotherapy or counselling in a setting which happens to contain other people, the group members.

This chapter is divided into two parts. In Part 1 we look at the aspects of group-analytic thinking which are based in individual psychoanalytic and psychodynamic theory and practice. In Part 2 we use the example of Georgina (and others) to think about how the group can help an individual.

Part 1: Drawing Ideas from Psychoanalysis

Psychoanalytic and psychodynamic work rests on the basic understanding that there is a hidden part of each person's mind, the **unconscious**, which remains inaccessible so that the person can maintain a picture of himself which he finds acceptable, even though on the surface he may believe that he desperately wants to change it. A familiar example of this is a fat woman who is convinced that she wants to be thin and yet it never happens; rather than assuming that she lacks will power, a psychodynamic approach suggests that she has found this to be the best compromise she can reach between her unconscious conflicts and desires and her conscious mind.

CASE EXAMPLE

Angela has tried to lose weight with no success. She recognises that there may be some underlying emotional causes. As an adolescent she felt torn between her parents' very strict moral and sexual code and the more liberal behaviour of her friends. Unable to confront her conflicts and her intensely ambivalent feelings towards her parents, she withdrew from social life with her peers using the excuse that she was too fat for anyone to want to go out with.

As in Angela's case, the chosen solution appears to be the only way of dealing with frightening desires, unpalatable thoughts and irresolvable conflicts, but gives rise to symptoms or ways of living which render the person at least unhappy and at worst incapacitated.

Freud (1974) found by using the method of **free association**, asking his patients to speak about whatever passed through their minds, whether or not it seemed to make sense, within the bounded framework of the analytic session, he gained access to unconscious material. Looking at a patient's dreams and other unguarded communications such as slips of the tongue and jokes was similarly revealing. Freud came to recognise that it was the way in which the relationship between the analyst and the patient developed which allowed this unconscious material to come to consciousness through the patient's feelings and fantasies about the analyst. The analyst tried to be as neutral as possible to allow the patient to transfer his feelings (of which he had previously been unconscious) onto the analyst. These feelings turned out to originate in past relationships with people who were highly significant for the patient, often family members. This process was termed **transference**.

The three basic ideas which Foulkes brought from psychoanalysis, the unconscious, free association and the transference relationship, all play an important part within group-analytic thinking and are applicable to groups which do not specifically aim to interpret unconscious communications. Working within a group, Foulkes pointed out that free association happens between group members rather than within the individual; similarly, he found that group members had transferences to each other as well as to the group conductor.

In individual analysis (and in psychodynamic therapy and coun-selling) the analyst's role has been to interpret the transference (although with the increasing awareness and use of the **countertransference**, this has changed to a more interactional model). In the group, the situation is more complex. Pines (1993, p. 99) describes the group conductor's interpretive tasks: 'S/he is a contributor both to individual work with a member of the group and also to the dynamics of the group as a whole.'

Within the group there are two broad categories of interpretation. The first is similar to that in the individual therapy setting, being addressed to a particular group member or exploring the transference onto the conductor. The second facilitates communication between group members, metaphorical *speakers of different languages* (see Pines, 1998). Direct interpretation of transference material does not have the central role in group therapy that it has in individual work. (All of these processes are illustrated in Chapter 4.)

Countertransference was initially seen as the analyst's response to the patient's transference; an indication of something which the analyst had not worked through herself. Group analysis, like psychoanalysis, now has a different view of countertransference; the conductor monitors her own responses to the group interaction to get a *reading* of the unconscious processes in the group. While this aspect of the therapist's response to a patient or group must be distinguished from other aspects of the therapist's responses, as the observer did in Chapter 1, there is an increasing emphasis on using the therapist's experience as a form of response to the patient's or group's unconscious communications. This takes place through the mechanism of **projective identification**.

Developmental models

Psychoanalysis provides some models of individual development which enable us to make sense of what has gone wrong for the men and women who approach us for treatment.

Within psychoanalysis there are many different schools with their own variants of a developmental account: we present a mainstream position for group-analytic therapists emphasising the importance of the interaction between the infant and its carers. This suggests that the roots of an individual's problems lie in his relationships with others with the inference that treatment in the interactive situation of the group will have particular therapeutic value.

Foulkes thought that Freud had provided the basis for a theory of individual development which recognised the importance of society's impact on the individual's psyche. According to Freud, the individual has the task of sorting out the conflicts between the instincts and society's attempts to restrict their expression (initially through the family) and the limits posed by the actual physical environment. Growing up meant addressing these painful and often seemingly irresolvable conflicts. However, some of Foulkes' psychoanalytic contemporaries highlighted the role of the relationship between the infant and others in forming the personality, rather than the significance of the struggle between the infant's instincts and the ways in which society needed to crush or modify them. Therapy was needed when something went wrong with the development of the capacity to relate to others. What group therapy offers is a situation in which the origins of difficulties in relationships can be explored. Thus developmental theories which focus on the importance of the earliest interaction between infant and mother have, in recent years, been used within a group-analytic approach (see Harwood and Pines, 1998; Marrone and Diamond, 1998). From the wealth of psychoanalytic theory we have chosen Winnicott, Bowlby and a brief account of Bion's concept of containment as a starting point.

Bowlby (1979) posited the further instinct of attachment between mother and infant, which he saw as being independent of, for instance, the sexual instinct. Winnicott emphasised the importance of the environment for the development of the infant. Winnicott (1964, p. 88) wrote: 'There is no such thing as a baby – meaning that if you set out to describe a baby you will find that you are describing a baby and someone. A baby cannot exist alone, but is essentially part of a relationship.'

Winnicott's account of early development

Winnicott introduced the concept of **holding** to describe the particular way in which the mother of the newborn infant provides him with the kind of illusory environment which he needs. The environment can facilitate the infant's development. Winnicott described the physical expression of holding through the actual physical care and handling but pointed out that this care represents and expresses something more. He wrote about 'the total environmental provision prior to the concept of living with' (1960, p. 43). He said that the reliability of the mother's care must 'imply the mother's empathy' (p. 48). 'It is perhaps the only way the mother can show the infant her love' (p. 49). Within this holding environment, the baby can gradually develop his sense of his own continuity. If the baby does not feel securely held, he experiences an impingement and in his unintegrated state, without the psychic resources to deal with intrusion, the baby experiences itself as annihilated. To protect itself from such an experience, the baby will develop a *false self* as a shield for the incipient *true self*, the developing ego.

If all goes well, as the ego develops the mother recognises that the baby no longer needs her to respond empathically; that the baby has enough of a sense of being inside his skin to begin to ask for things from a person who exists inside a separate skin. Hoggett (1992) explained that the mother's task is to create the illusion for the infant of being in the womb, but this is translated into a social form: a relationship between two people. The baby is then 'let down' gently to discover that he is actually a separate person from his mother.

The baby begins to discover that he does not have control over the world. He needs to test out his environment to see if it can withstand his growing strength. It is only if he really tries to destroy 'the object' (the other crucial person involved) and finds that it can survive that he knows for sure that he and the other person can exist separately and relate to each other. This knowledge and confidence allows for the development of the ability to imagine, to behave 'as if' something were the case, while knowing that it is not. Winnicott called this the capacity to **play**, connecting it to artistic creativity and to creativity in the spontaneous interaction between people.

Many people who come for therapy are unable to play, dominated by a need to live in a fantasy world in which they are still the omnipotent baby, or by the need to please and comply rather than to live. They may be what Winnicott called *anti-social* as a way of showing others that all is not well within.

Winnicott's terms, holding and playing, are often used to describe what happens in a group setting and can help us to understand the plight of individual group members. Georgina's lack of early holding affected her psychological development, making her compliant and unable to relate spontaneously, living her life through ministering to the needs of others. When this strategy could no longer help her to avoid feeling pain and loss she developed physical symptoms as an alternative to expressing her feelings.

Attachment theory

Bowlby's attachment theory provides another model for understanding the individual's difficulties in dealing with separation, mourning and loss, incorporating the importance of the social environment. He suggested that attachment behaviour represents a particular biologically based system that does not derive from other instinctual behaviour. That is, the infant's attachment to his caregiver is a bond in its own right and not something secondary to the need to reduce certain drives. Attachment behaviour is not *cupboard love*; it is a primary instinct with the aim of being close to a mother figure. The infant's experience of attachment formed in his relationship with his mother shapes his psychological development. Through satisfactory attachment to the mother he develops a secure-enough base. If the mother is available, her outer predictability becomes inner certainty. The child will feel safe enough to leave that base to explore the world, which the child must do if he is to grow and learn.

Actual experiences give rise to **representational models** of the environment and of the self which tend to persist in life. When an individual forms a bond with another person (such as the boss, the partner or the therapist), the person is assimilated to an existing model of the self or a parent, in spite of evidence to the contrary. He will do, and expect to be done by, according to the models that have been learned from experience. Georgina's representational model may have been formed by her cold relationship with her mother, expecting that others would treat her similarly and would only accept her if she helped. Georgina had no **secure base** through attachment to her mother and unconsciously continued to behave as if others would relate to her as her family had done.

Bowlby argues that a therapist must enable the patient to consider, in detail, how his present modes of perceiving and dealing with emotionally significant persons, including the therapist, may be influenced and perhaps distorted by experiences in childhood and adolescence with his parents, which affect him in the present. Bowlby emphasises the importance of recalling the child's actual experience in therapy rather than his fantasy life. Within the therapeutic relationship a secure base is established from which the patient can be encouraged to explore himself and his relationships. In the back and forth relationship between a secure base and exploration of the way he relates to others (including the therapist) the patient recognises how patterns of relating may be the product of real experiences, leading to representational models which may no longer be appropriate. Establishing a secure base with the therapist may be difficult but gradually the patient finds that this grows, enabling him to have better relationships in his everyday life.

When a group's aim is to make conscious and work with its members' difficulties in relating to others, it needs to provide a special kind of space; one in which the members can safely become aware of the ways in which their present modes of relating to others are outmoded and do not correspond to their present experience. A group with more specific aims, such as the group for agoraphobia described in Chapter 1, also needs safety. The group needs to provide a **holding environment** (in Winnicott's language) or a **secure base** (the term used in attachment theory).

Another psychoanalytic concept used to explain the particular properties of a group is to speak of it as a **container**. This derives from Bion's term, describing the mother's earliest function in relation to the infant as being that of **containment**. The infant evacuates the bad elements of his experience, which he cannot process, into the mother. If the mother is psychically available she detoxifies these elements for the infant and returns them to the infant in a manageable form. She contains the infant's experience so that he can bear it and reclaim it. Often the terms holding and containing are used interchangeably and imprecisely. They do refer to different processes and to different accounts of psychological development (James, 1994). In the group, holding parallels the mother's physical caretaking of the newborn infant and may be expressed in the emotional significance of the conductor's concern with the practical arrangements for the group. Containment refers to the group's capacity to process feelings which in everyday life may be too frightening to enter the group members' consciousness.

LEARNING POINTS

- **Unconscious** processes are to be found in all types of group, whether the group aims to explore them or not.
- One way of gaining access to the unconscious is through asking a person to say whatever comes into his mind or to **free associate**. Within a group-analytic group members speaking freely to each other is seen as the equivalent of free association. In a group which is more structured group members may say things in an associative way reflecting unconscious thoughts.
- The earliest childhood relationships have a profound effect on later personal development and this will, in turn, affect relationships within a group setting.
- Early relationships can be **transferred** onto a therapist or, in a group, onto the group conductor or other group members, so that old relationships are replayed in the present. When this is understood it can be used therapeutically.
- Similarly the therapist or the group conductor's thoughts and feelings, which are evoked by what they experience, the **counter-transference,** can provide an important way of accessing hidden or unconscious material.

■ Two ideas which are taken from psychoanalytic study of early mother–infant relationships and applied to groups are **holding** and **containing**.

■ The idea of the relationship between mother/carer and child providing a **secure base** is taken from attachment theory and applied to the experience in a group.

Part 2: Applying Group Concepts to the Experience of the Individual

Foulkes' view of how group analysis could help the individual

Foulkes was predisposed to believe that a form of therapy which involved more than two people meeting might be helpful because he saw therapy in a group as embodying his belief that environmental and social issues are as formative as internal emotional experience on the child's psychological development. He was influenced by the experience of the rise of fascism in Germany and the dramatic change in his own life when he came to England as a refugee in the 1930s. By concretising his ideas in the group setting, Foulkes was unable fully to realise the implications of a social perspective for psychotherapy (see Dalal, 1998).

Foulkes described the individual's disturbance as 'an incompatibility between the individual and his original group' (1948, p. 165) by which he meant both the family and the community at large. The family was, 'precipitated in the innermost core of the human mind, incorporated into the child's growing ego and superego' (p. 15) acting as a mediator between the child and society, imposing on the child 'the restrictions which society demands' (1938, p. 80). Believing that psychoanalysis could show how communication from community to family to child takes place, Foulkes wrote: 'Individual psychotherapy is thus a form of group psychotherapy' (Foulkes and Anthony, 1957, p. 27). He meant that whether he had one or eight patients in the room he had a family and a wider group of people in his mind:

> We have to deal with the restoration of this disturbed communication.
> (Foulkes and Anthony, 1964, p. 28)

Applying this to Georgina, on joining the group she expected to give an account of *her problem* while everyone listened, chimed in with similar stories, relevant questions or good advice. Alternatively she thought she would have her turn to speak with the therapist who would ask her probing questions, while others listened, gaining from what they could relate to in her story. Both of these pictures are based on the idea that group therapy is about doing individual therapy within a group setting. What actually happens is somewhat different.

Foulkes' vision of how a group could be therapeutic was neither to do individual work with an empathic group audience, nor to look at the group *as a whole* and try to understand it as if it were itself an organism relating to him as group conductor. Foulkes demanded something very difficult of group therapists, namely that they keep in mind both what is happening for the group as a whole and what is happening for particular individuals. What was crucial was the dynamic relationship between these two perspectives and indeed between individuals, subgroups and the whole group, which is illustrated in the group in Chapter 4. He derived this approach from **Gestalt** psychology, drawing on the idea that the whole picture, experience or group could only be understood by looking at the relationship between the **figure**, the image in the foreground of the picture, or the protagonist in a particular group, and what was going on in the background or the **ground**. The example he gave was of a person leaving the group:

> This must be understood from the person's point of view as well as from the rest of the group's point of view and is in fact a result of the interaction. (Foulkes, 1957, p. 21)

Foulkes drew an analogy between the group and a jigsaw puzzle. A person in isolation is like a single piece of the puzzle which has no meaning unless it can be inserted into the jigsaw. When an individual joins a therapy group she tries to reconstruct the original jigsaw of her own family, shaping the other pieces (people) to fit.

Initially Georgina behaves as if everyone in the group needs her help which she appears to give willingly but other group members notice that she is habitually late for the group. When challenged, she says that being late has nothing to do with her being helpful. She has something to offer as an experienced woman and she can see that the group conductor is not going to provide many answers.

Georgina demonstrates her shape as a jigsaw piece, assuming that the jigsaw has a suitable space for her. In her *original* jigsaw, Georgina was the eldest child of a large family whose mother resented Georgina's conception which had trapped her into an early marriage. Applying the concepts outlined in this chapter, we can see that Georgina did not have a good experience of holding or containment by her mother. Mother and baby had attachment difficulties. She developed an anxious inverted attachment leading to compulsive caregiving, which hid her own yearning for love and her rage. Her close relationship with her father appeared to end at puberty and she identified with her mother's grievances against her father.

In the group she behaves as if the male group conductor is not there; if she is on time she will continue a conversation when he comes into the room. Since she knows he provides no answers she writes him off. She is replaying a familiar scenario: the jigsaw she is going to fit into originated in her childhood and has been repeated in her marriage. At first she cannot be persuaded to look at herself in a different way. Her identity is confirmed when she is helping others. She can only operate on psychological *automatic pilot*.

She listens to the other group members saying strange things to each other. Often they say whatever comes into their heads even if it appears not to follow on. They laugh, cry, joke, criticise, tease each other and even include the group conductor. Georgina feels lost. She does not know what to do or how to be. One day something makes her burst into tears: another woman, Rita, arrives rain soaked in the group and Derek takes off his jacket and offers it to her to keep her warm. Georgina's tears express a mixture of envy of Rita and sadness about her own unfulfilled longings. Georgina realises that underneath her capable front she misses being cared for.

A piece of Georgina's jigsaw was wearing down as she started to communicate in the group.

Georgina describes her own experience of the group as follows.

When I went into the group I thought I would get some help with my problems. I talked about how I keep forgetting the simplest thing but although the others were sympathetic and another person had the same difficulty, no one had any helpful suggestions; especially not the therapist. Well, I kept going, feeling a bit frustrated and I don't know quite how it happened but one day I found myself crying in the group. I realised I had strong feelings about different people in the group and somehow it made me feel a bit better after the sessions – not always – but sometimes.

Garland (1982, p. 6) described this experience:

There is a period in which an individual's presenting problem is accepted by the group. However, after a while, mysteriously the presenting problem is dropped ...in favour of something which is not the problem, not what the individual patient believed he joined the group to involve himself with – it is dropped in favour of passionate discussion of and involvement with the shifting roles, relationships and behavioural communications which make up the system of the group itself.

She suggests that it is through attending to the *non-problem* (what is happening in the group) that the 'individual becomes a member of an alternative system to the one in which his symptom... was generated and maintained'.

For Georgina her original **system**, her family (and her marriage) reinforced her denial of her own needs, the pain she suffered and her inability to protest. Through becoming part of a new system, the group, in which people related in different ways, she discovered what had happened to her and began to communicate her own experience.

What keeps the group together?

A picture is emerging of how and why therapy in a group can be helpful to an individual. Foulkes wrote about the group in terms of figure and ground, and being a jigsaw puzzle, while Garland refers to the group as a system. Other ideas of the group which have been mentioned are the provision of a holding environment, a secure base and the group offering a containing environment. The questions which still need answering are what holds the group together and what kinds of psychological mechanisms enable a person to move from the autism of the symptom to communication in the group.

Foulkes conceived of the group as developing a **matrix** as a way of talking about the complex relationships between individuals, subgroups and the whole group. The matrix can be understood as the common shared ground which determines the meaning and significance of all that happens within the group. At a simple level, the implication is that anything which happens within the boundary of the group is meaningful for the group. Each individual represents a nodal point within the complex network of relationships which exists within the group.

Group-analytic thinking also draws on another concept from psychoanalysis, projective identification, to explain how the unconscious communication between group members takes place within the group matrix. When a group member is unaware that he feels angry himself and tells another person she is angry we term this unconscious process **projection**. He is ridding himself of a feeling he cannot tolerate but is conscious of seeing the anger in the other person. Projective identification takes this one stage further. The initially angry person uses the other person as a vehicle without being aware that there is any connection between them. A new group member appears unperturbed by his arrival in the group and behaves as if he were the co-therapist. Meanwhile, the group therapist finds herself paralysed and confused. She realises afterwards that the new group member may have been confused and unconsciously used her as a receptacle for his feelings. In a group the aim is to move from projective communication to conscious verbal communication.

An example of the matrix and projective processes in groups

CASE EXAMPLE

Vikram wonders whether to leave his therapy group. He can't decide whether the group members and conductor are encouraging him to replay his childhood experiences as the butt of others' needs and anger. Are they bullying him to stay in the group for their own ulterior motives? The consensus in the group is that he is mistaken and is running away from the place where he could resolve some of his difficulties in relating to others. The group is in turmoil and so is Vikram; he cries and cannot make up his mind.

The group conductor sees that the group could help Vikram but the fact that everyone is lined up against him makes her suspicious. Looking at it from Vikram's viewpoint, as one *node* in the group matrix, he finds it hard to participate fully in the group without *feeling* that he is being subservient. Neither of Vikram's parents could brook conflict or offer their son a solid sense of growing up as an Indian man within British society. Vikram's personal dilemma was intimately affected by his country's history, its traumatic impact economically, socially and psychologically on his family, leaving him fearful of taking risks which might repeat his family's losses. Moreover, he experienced painful humiliation as an Indian child growing up in Britain. Even in the apparently liberal group, Vikram might be being made use of in a subtle way. One of the psychological effects of racism is that white people may unconsciously use black and Asian people as a dumping ground for their own unwanted emotions.

The conductor realises that other group members feel humiliated and fear conflict. The majority confidently express the desire to work in the group which is one side of Vikram's dilemma while he is isolated, indecisive, troubled and weak. The group conductor sees how projective identification is used by several group members unconsciously to rid themselves of unwanted feelings of neediness and inferiority into Vikram. Vikram is a willing recipient of the other group members' projections; he identifies because he does indeed feel inferior, needy and remains the patient in the group, receiving attention and not confronting his fears of being a stronger person. The group forms itself into the jigsaw puzzle which has a space for the old Vikram jigsaw piece.

Looking at the matrix, it seems that issues of ambivalence towards parents, fears of dependency and difficulties in separation abound; the group has selected Vikram to carry some of these issues because his personal history and his being Asian both predispose him for this role. He accepts it. Thus the social context enters into the daily workings of the group. The conductor will now look for ways of helping the group to understand what is happening in the matrix so that further work can take place.

LEARNING POINTS

■ A group member can rediscover and work through unresolved repressed conflicts (which may have led to problematic symptoms) through the interaction within the group.

■ The group conductor needs to keep both the individual and the group in mind and try to understand the interaction between the two.

■ In the group each group member tries to impose her version of family relationships onto the group. Gradually she discovers that others do not see the world in this way and she begins to adjust her vision in the light of what she sees.

■ The group does not help its members by talking about their presenting problems but rather through the process of being a member of the group and participating in the group communication.

■ **Projective identification** is a psychoanalytic concept which can help to explain how unconscious communication takes place in the group so that one person can influence what another is feeling without either of them being aware of it. The group aims to move from projective processes to verbal communication.

■ How people relate to each other in groups is affected not only by their personal background but also by social and historical factors.

3

Growing a Group

Introduction

The line drawn around a group, creating a **boundary**, makes creativity possible. Rothenberg (1988) argues that in psychotherapy, as in *any* creative process, a focus on the formal aspects of the material – the words, notes, colours, objects or mathematical formulae – contributes to the creative content of the work. The therapist must be mindful of how form and content interrelate and complement each other. Exclusive concern with content leaves us out of touch and uncontained; exclusive concern with form can simply be making an issue out of group members' lateness.

The focus on boundaries may appear obsessive and frustrating – but their usefulness in creating and maintaining the group as a therapeutic space soon becomes apparent. The relatively fixed structure of the group holds people together, in two senses: the **outer predictability** of a setting, a set time and place can lead to an **inner sense of being held** in a safe place – like the holding environment provided for the infant (Winnicott, 1971). A good-enough **external** holding environment becomes an **internalised** holding environment. The former is conscious and concerns the form and structure of the group; the latter is largely unconscious and is to do with the social traffic of projections and introjections concerning the external holding environment itself. By **setting** the stage for therapy and by attending to its boundaries, the conductor develops this important holding function of group therapy. She interests group members in how boundary incidents, such as latenesses, have meaning for the latecomer and the rest of the group: form and content are dynamically related.

As a group begins to feel safely held, it can develop a space for thinking, in which members are contained. Bion (1962) wrote about the way a mother contacts the infant's state of mind and, through her attention and support, helps the infant to develop psychologically – as if her mind were a container for the child. For Winnicott (1971), it is within a safe space that we start to play creatively and begin to use symbols which in themselves provide further containment. Thus the importance of the setting and boundaries of any group goes beyond the purely practical. Dynamic growth and development in the group have humble origins. Group analysis refers to this work in building groups as **dynamic administration** to emphasise the crucial relationship between the practical and the dynamic. Groups highlight the need for boundary setting to create the pre-conditions for a therapeutic space to develop which, in a simplified form, is familiar to the individual therapist or counsellor.

Growing a Group

The group conductor's list

Metaphorically the group starts life as the merest twinkle in the eye of the conductor. This chapter goes through the conductor's list of things to be done to transform that twinkle into the reality of a group with therapeutic potential.

THE CONDUCTOR'S LIST

1. Whom to have in the group.
2. How it will help the members.
3. Is a co-conductor needed?
4. Setting the group up: finding the space/relating to the organisation/ selecting the members.
5. Addressing the members' and the conductor's anxieties; preparing them all for the group.

The therapist (or group conductor) decides whether she wants a co-conductor. The conductor defines the group's aims, which affect the type of group and its duration. She ensures that the group is established within a facilitating environment. Once the pre-conditions are set, she will select and prepare the group's membership. She will prepare herself and her co-conductor recognising the inherent anxieties, which will help them to survive and reduce their defensiveness.

**Whom are you going to work with? What sort of group will
help and how?**

The group conductor may start a group to accommodate existing
clients/patients or may decide that a certain type of group would be a
useful service to offer and will seek referrals.

A therapist becomes aware of a need among a group of people where
she works. It may be expressed as a deficiency (lack of social skills), as
a symptom (anxiety to be managed), as an unacceptable behaviour to be
controlled (eating, anger or sexual abuse), or where there is a potential
for growth.

The potential members may be looking for therapy or a therapeutic
group; they may be sent (as on probation); they may just want their
symptoms or difficulties to be removed. Whitaker (1985) suggests the
therapist considers what is the **preoccupying concern** of the potential
group member. There will be some issue, life event or responsibility
that dominates the person's life. She also describes the importance of
clarifying the **frontier** between the skills and resources the person has
and those he does not yet possess. He will need these skills to resolve
the issues that emanate from the preoccupying concern. This may
clarify what the group member might want to achieve and how a group
might help him do this. As the appropriate therapeutic approach
emerges, the rationale can be discussed with him.

The conductor's decisions about what sort of people she wants to
offer a group to, with what expectations, will determine the decisions
she takes about what kind of line to draw around her group. Her line will
include the length of the sessions, the duration of the therapy, what sort
of therapy it is, and where and when it takes place.

A group may be assembled around the similarities or the apparent
differences of its members: a **homogeneous** group or a **heterogeneous**
group; it may be a **slow-open** ongoing group, in which a member may
leave when he is ready and be replaced by a new member; or a **closed**
group with a fixed membership and time limit. It may not be possible
to introduce new members into a structured group with organised
sessions so the number of sessions should be limited. A closed group
may last for a *term* up to an *academic year*. If it needs to continue for
more than a year, setting a time limit at the beginning is questionable
since life events may intrude, making it difficult to keep a full group.
Given the work involved in setting up a new group it may be more
effective to have a slow-open group, even if it is for a homogeneous
population. One NHS psychotherapy department has a slow-open

group for people who have been sexually abused but has developed a culture where most members do not remain for more than 18 months. Slow-open heterogeneous groups allow the member to stay for as long as he needs to achieve some significant change. There are also external considerations such as the group conductor's own future plans or the availability of funding.

What we stress here is that the decisions about the type of group and its boundaries are made, bearing in mind group issues and the members' needs, before the conductor looks for group members. Recognising that the form and structure of the group will influence its content and process implies that drawing a line around the practical life of the group creates a boundary that has *meaning* for its members.

There are many ways of using groups to help people. The group-analytic approach is particularly mindful of how the structure of therapy suggests and generates its content; and it *uses* this observation therapeutically. We saw in Chapter 2 how the family structure forms a jigsaw piece that contrives to shape its social surroundings to its own contours of meaning. However, it is not so much that a human being is a thing of a set shape: rather, it is as if human *being* is a verb; behind the structure of the family/group or the jigsaw piece/personality is the *process* of making meaning. The conductor's list does not merely consist of chores to be done before the real work of conducting sessions starts. A trainee may spend months in supervision struggling to find appropriate members for her group in an unwelcoming organi-sation, only to say in exasperation: 'I wish this stuff was all over and I could just do some therapy!' An understandable feeling – but work on 'this stuff' is vital. Many problems brought to supervision are linked to 'the stuff' the therapist did not attend to before the group met for the first session.

Once the group conductor has decided on the type of group she wants to run, for what sort of patients, with what aims, and for how long, she needs to turn her attention to the setting within which she will conduct her group.

Planning and Negotiating within the Organisation

Setting up the group within an organisation

Setting up the group involves thinking about the external space – both physical and psychic.

The external psychic space, or **network**, needs to be supportive of the group. The aims of the group should fit as closely as possible with the aims of the network. The conductor should have *control* over the therapeutic space, but this must be negotiated within the external psychic space of her host network.

CASE EXAMPLE

> A therapist in a community mental health team recently completed a groupwork course, and wants to start a longer-term analytic group. The therapist is willing to work in her own time, furthering her personal interests outside her contracted work, but the person in charge of the mental health centre has reservations about a group which does not fit in with his organisation's primary task which is to deal with the throughput of patients, offering a maximum of 6 months' treatment. The therapist thinks he is being resistant to her new proposal and feels tempted to go ahead and start the group.

However, a group can only have a protected therapeutic space if it has the backing of those in the surrounding network. Whitaker (1985) argues for the importance of analysing the power and authority structures and the flow of communication within the organisation in which the proposed group will run. She suggests: 'When problems arise within organizations and institutions these typically have to do with imbalances with respect to the relationship between task, power, information and responsibility' (p. 106). The would-be conductor must explain her plans clearly, negotiate an agreement at the appropriate levels – starting at the top – and try to understand any organisational *resistance* to them in the spirit of aiming for a win/win solution. The network wins if the group helps it with its overall task and the conductor wins if she is confident that it will receive referrals and not be disrupted by external events. Talking face to face about her concerns and theirs, with room for negotiation and compromise, may achieve her goal. However, for any particular group there will be some basic structures over which there can be no compromise. Similarly, if an organisation acquiesces to an unwanted group it can become a dumping ground for patients/clients who may not want or be able to make use of the group; or there may be no referrals.

While necessary, it is not sufficient to secure agreement *at the top*. The conductor needs to develop a daily working relationship with a clinic administrator or departmental secretary based on an understanding of the group and attention to practical details. The administrator can tell the group conductor when the cleaners come in, when the heating goes off and how to make sure that the conductor can get in. Just as important is someone who will reliably take messages from members *and* make sure the conductor gets them before each session.

The clinical example graphically describes the disasters that arise if such issues are not adequately addressed.

CASE EXAMPLE

One of the authors ran a group as an outsider without making this link properly, and found the group room empty one night apart from a decorator's ladder and some pots of paint. Another occasion found him halfway up a drainpipe heading for what looked like an unlocked window, in an otherwise impenetrable and deserted building, in full view of the early arrivals to his group. The same group turned up another night to discover that their room was now the secretary's office, after an unrelated row she had had with the boss whom the conductor had negotiated the group with in the first place.

Communicating across the boundary of the group

Therapists can foster envious curiosity by their secrecy and exclusiveness. Providing a secure base for therapy does not imply having a siege mentality. If the host organisation is ultimately responsible for the group members (who are their patients, clients or users), there will be some requirement to share information which can be negotiated with both the organisation and the members. For instance, if the conductor is clear that she will be writing to a group member's psychiatrist in broad terms about his therapy at agreed intervals, but that she will not tell his mother what he has been talking about when she phones (as she does), then everyone will know where they stand. Most importantly for therapy, the patient will. Similarly in a group for mothers of children on the 'at risk' register in a social services department it was important for the groupworkers to tell the mothers that they would inform the relevant social workers if anything arose which might jeopardise a child's safety.

The degree of privacy needed relates to the type of group: in an analytic therapy group, if members are to speak freely and intimately, they must feel that what is said will not be used and abused elsewhere. Within a staff group inevitably what is said in a group session will be discussed outside. Sometimes group members who demand rigid rules about confidentiality are unconsciously attempting to control the group. A group which has watertight confidentiality has an impermeable boundary which (as well as keeping secrets within the group) prevents information and energy coming in so that the group may stagnate. Like many boundary issues, confidentiality should be discussed as issues arise.

In the first session of the group described in Chapter 4, a member speaks about having broken confidentiality at work, and this theme preoccupies the group. Perhaps this is because there is a high level of anxiety in the group created by the group conductor's rather wobbly boundary setting.

Another professional's request for information about a group member gives rise to ethical issues; it is also an opportunity for the conductor to model an approach by raising it in the group. The appropriate response can be agreed with both the specific member and the other group members.

It is simpler if the conductor restricts her role to that of expert in group therapy. If she is a group member's psychiatrist or key worker, she should shed this pre-existing role. A colleague might be persuaded to take it on in exchange for a returned favour. In the social services group described earlier the role of groupworker was separated from the role of statutory social worker for the mothers or their children. If the conductor has to maintain dual roles she must make them part of the therapeutic group process. When she is the key worker, how will the review process become part of the group?

If concurrent individual and group therapy are offered as part of an in-patient or day patient programme, perhaps the conductor should be everyone's or no one's individual therapist, otherwise there will be too much scope for the group to avoid working at its task through splitting, competition for individual attention and jealousy. The conductor is trying to balance the needs of the individual within the external space as she finds it, but with the ultimate aim of setting up the group as a secure base along group-analytic lines.

Defining the Therapist's Task in the Group

Clarity of the reason for the group, what is the expected outcome and how this is achieved results in:

- defining the structure
- defining the therapeutic approach
- informing the therapist's style and actions
- influence on the assessment and selection of members.

The group setting

Alongside the conductor's negotiations with the organisation to create an external space which allows the internal space of the group to be explored independently of outside factors, she must also decide how this internal space can be organised to facilitate the group's aims. As with the other practicalities these are not side issues. Foulkes (1975) dignified them with the term the **conditions set**. Where these conditions are not relevant to all groups, alternatives are considered:

1. When the aim of the group is to provide a protected space for exploring fantasies, encouraging play and trying out different ways of relating to each other, *the group members should be strangers to one another*. Then what transpires between group members cannot have direct consequences on their relationships with each other outside the group. Where the aim of the group is to develop outside group connections between group members (for example, a group for new mothers) or where the group's aim is to explore relationships between people who already have connections (for example, a staff group for ward staff) this does not apply.

2. *The mode of joining the group must be clearly established.* Members need to know what form of group they are joining and whether and how new members will be admitted. In a closed group everyone joins at the same time and no new members are admitted, with everyone leaving at the end. Dropouts can cause problems for such groups, but carefully selected, time-limited and theme-centred groups can work well. In the slow-open group people who leave (ready or not) are replaced. Arrivals and departures are experienced in a consistent setting.

3. *Making the room suit the group.* Careful thought needs to be given to the practical arrangement of the group room. While Foulkes described the sort of room needed for an analytic group in some detail, each conductor will make her own compromises between what is necessary and what is desirable. Different groups have their own requirements: an art therapy group will need provision for painting or work with clay, including the materials, plenty of space and floor and furnishings which are not too easily damaged by messy materials.

4. *The group sits in a circle.* The circle is the nearest we can get to a face-to-face situation where everyone can see everyone else. This is not possible around a boardroom table. Also, in a circle, everyone is equal and no one is at the head of the table. The circle has symbolic potential.

5. *Members are free to sit on any vacant chair in the circle.* Seating patterns then build up in the group mind, can be seen as communications and talked about in the context of the total patterning of relationships in the group. The conductor either puts out a chair for each group member or as many chairs as there are people expected. If the group is a drop-in the conductor will need ingenuity to ensure that new arrivals can find a seat without early arrivals having to sit in the middle of a sea of chairs.

6. *The conductor decides how many members to have in the group.* Foulkes said that one person is alone, two form a pair and three are, in a sense, the beginning of a group. Group dynamics emerge and group balance can be used as a therapeutic technique (discussed later) when there are at least five members. Then the group begins to offer a diversity of similarities and differences for members to draw upon, more closely representing the social norm. Six to nine is seen as optimal for group-analytic therapy. Above nine the group process limits the therapeutic potential for the individual, while an experiential group, focusing on group process, can be larger. There is a marked reduction in interactions between members at a group size of nine and another at a membership of seventeen (see Yalom, 1995). As size increases, some people continue to say a lot, but others become wallflowers. Much can be learned about unconscious group processes in larger groups. Where groups mainly work doing structured exercises in pairs or small groups the total membership can be larger.

7. *The conductor decides when the group takes place, how frequently it meets, for how long and for how many sessions.* The group time should be acceptable to the conductor and her group members, remembering that it cannot easily be altered. Often groups are set up outside normal working hours to accommodate the needs of the conductor, the host institution and the prospective group members. The therapy interferes with the *social time* of members and therapists alike and careful thought must be given to which times will be least intrusive for everyone.

Foulkes regarded once a week to be the minimum frequency for an analytic group. He found twice-weekly groups interesting but did not think they shortened the duration of the therapy. In the public sector most groups are weekly for practical reasons. Starting on training courses, therapy has been offered using blocks of groups. The group meets at longer, but regular, intervals (for example monthly or three-monthly) having several sessions in an intensive period of a few days (see Behr and Hearst 1990). This method is used now by some group analysts (for further information see Chapter 9 and the clinical service of the Institute of Group Analysis).

The weekly session normally lasts an hour and a half, but will be longer in psychodrama and some activity groups. The clinical consensus is that a shorter session (of an hour or less) does not give enough time for the group to warm up, whereas the warm-up period will expand to fill the space available in a much longer session (of two hours or more), with diminishing returns and tiredness all round. The conductor can safely compromise with an hour and a quarter, but must establish an agreed length of meeting time. The overall duration of the group depends upon its purpose and the extent to which it is part of a wider programme. Theme-centred groups will usually have a fixed duration as do structured groups.

This section on the setting has really been a counsel of perfection. Rewarding groups have surely been conducted in oddly shaped rooms with no windows, next to gurgling boilers. With gurgling or without gurgling? It will make a difference. Yet straying too far and too often from the counsel of perfection can overwhelm the boundary concept and undermine the therapeutic space. It is important to think about what sort of group it is you are creating.

Selecting the Members

Referrals

Many new conductors set up groups in a statutory environment, with referrals coming from other mental health professionals or from primary care (usually GPs). It is unusual for someone to be referred specifically for group therapy. A GP faced with a person with emotional problems is often hard pressed to know whether to refer him to a psychiatrist, a counsellor, a clinical psychologist or a psychotherapist, or whether this should be for individual or group therapy. Some GP practices do now employ counsellors (or psychologists) who will see a patient (usually for a limited number of sessions) and assess and refer him, if necessary.

Many people undertaking advanced training negotiate to set up their groups in a specialist service, where they can select from a pool of screened and assessed individuals. Others circulate information about a prospective group, asking for potential members. The response may include some appropriate referrals, some patients with whom their referrers have countertransference difficulties, plus some who would benefit from a different form of therapy. Having to solve problems such as these as if she were a comprehensive specialist service will demand that the new group conductor spends much time and thought on communicating with her referrers. With supervision, she will have a richer, but more difficult, learning experience than someone who is placed with the specialist service and has side-stepped the negotiation with the institution.

Whom to select?

Mullan and Rosenbaum (1978) remind us that we are looking at a person's *suitability* for group therapy in general and at their suitability for *this* group at this point in time. Most people who are thought likely to benefit from individual exploratory therapy will be suitable for an analytically orientated group. So part of assessing for a group placement is essentially the same as for individual therapy (see Brown and Pedder, 1991) but the questions are formulated in terms of the group experience. We can think about four main questions.

1. Can the person reflect psychologically and see his problem in interpersonal terms?
2. Is his motivation directed towards interpersonal insight and change?
3. Will he be able to co-operate, share and be open with others? Does he expect them to be able to help?
4. Group therapy challenges defences, but will it shatter this person's? His capacity to form and sustain relationships and his *ego strength* are the salient issues here.

The group conductor meeting a prospective group member sees whether he can translate the presenting difficulties into a description of the way people relate to each other. If the patient cannot be encouraged away from seeing his difficulties in terms of a compulsion or an addiction, without reference to his past or present emotional experience, he is probably not ready for an analytic group.

She wants to know whether the prospective patient has a sense of his own contribution to his difficulties or whether he is determined to complain about his symptoms and blame them on others. If he can see that he has some part to play in his difficulties he will be interested to see what happens between him and other group members and will want their feedback. If not, other group members may become receptacles for his negative projections with little hope of a developing dialogue leading to insight. She will try to get a sense of whether her patient wants a 'magic cure' rather than personal change.

In looking at the prospective group member's background she will need to know whether he has had even one good relationship in the past which the therapy can build on. In the present she will be trying to assess whether he has the emotional resources to tolerate some pain and anxiety which will inevitably be stirred up in the group and will have to be borne between group sessions.

How does the conductor decide whether to offer a patient *group* therapy? We have suggested that the conductor needs to consider the person's capacity to see his problem in terms of his relationships to others, that he needs to be motivated to understand himself, to see the possibility of being helped by interacting with others and to be resilient enough to withstand the experience of relating to others in the group. Unfortunately these questions cannot be answered objectively and the therapist's answers are fallible. Assessment involves a conversation rather than an objective scientific procedure. The conductor is a participant observer: her *own* responses, her empathy, countertransference and sense of rapport are a rich source of data for gaining an understanding of the person's likely impact on the group, and vice versa. The prospective group member can imagine himself in a group setting which has particular emotional relevance for him.

Alternatively, the person may attend an assessment group (variously called **intake, diagnostic, holding, orientation** or **vestibule** groups) which has the dual function of assessment and preparation for group therapy proper. It is a live waiting list of people who are getting a taste of being in a group, and making their own assessment of the suitability of group therapy for themselves. Like individual assessment sessions, the process is really one of mutual appraisal.

In the interaction between conductor and patient (or within the assessment group) it is possible to look at the patient's misgivings and respond to them constructively, building a therapeutic alliance; a matter of preparation-cum-assessment. For instance, the conductor describes the group and asks the potential member how he feels about the prospect. He might say he feels worried about making a fool of himself. He would probably sit back at first, to see how the land lies, and gradually feel his way into things. He might be able to link this anxiety with earlier experiences in groups (maybe in his family). This would be a positive response to Question 1 in our list, making his anxiety intelligible to himself and the conductor. If he was unable to articulate his fear he might envisage a group with unthinkable alarm; the emotional unpredictability of a group would be too much of a threat to the self (see Joan in Chapter 7).

It is sometimes said that we should exclude from our groups those who find the group unbearable and those whom the group find unbearable: also that we should exclude those who cannot trust the group and those whom the group cannot trust. We have mentioned the highly threatened individual and the potentially disruptive one. Each of these individual and group considerations underlines the point that *the poor can get poorer* in group therapy. The disruptive person, who can only bring his problems to the group by enacting them (often in ways which disturb the group), becomes someone whom the group cannot accept or trust and he cannot take up the therapeutic opportunity which is being offered to him. He will probably leave reinforced in his belief that he cannot be held or contained (leaving the group to sort out what he has left behind, in his absence).

Discussion

Assessment involves taking a history and asking questions, but also involves building a relationship and providing a taste of psychotherapy. Yalom (1995) has summarised the clinical consensus about whom not to have in groups and advises us against having severely dysfunctional personality-disordered individuals and people with severe mental health problems, neurological conditions, learning difficulties or addictions in a mixed analytic-type group. Different kinds of group may be tailored to their particular concerns and aims. Others may be best helped to change using a different modality. When anxious to fill the last couple of places in a group, the conductor should resist the temptation to take in folk who would be better off in another (for example, briefer) therapy.

Rather than focusing on a list of exclusion factors, it seems more useful to remind ourselves of Whitaker's emphasis on the sheer versatility of groups as a medium for helping all sorts of people. We saw in Chapter 1 how groupwork can be mapped onto three dimensions with *type of patient* as one dimension, *purpose* as another and *type of group* the third. We have been considering groups aiming at personal change through psychotherapy (*purpose*) and which are set up as described in this chapter (*type of group*) to give them a better chance of achieving this aim.

For example, a bulimic person, preoccupied with bingeing and vomiting, may be best treated initially in a homogeneous group to develop the capacity to verbalise the emotions for which this behaviour is a metaphor (see Dana and Lawrence, 1988). Having a range of groups available means that patients will receive treatment in the most relevant group (*purpose*) and will not be forced into inappropriate groups. There are many possibilities once we have ascertained the person's frontier and preoccupying concern. A father whose child is terminally ill seeks therapy. At this point his preoccupying concern is common to other members of a group for parents of terminally ill children. They share their feelings and advice on how to cope with similar practicalities and experiences. Later an analytic group might be appropriate with an increasing need to explore in depth and fundamentally change his attitude to life, but now the preoccupying concern is never away from his thoughts.

For those in the group looking at developing appropriate sexual behaviour for people with learning difficulties there is a frontier, a 'just out of reach' area of interpersonal skills which, if acquired, would improve their relationships. This group is educational and practical; offering discussion and sharing of experiences. In the reminiscence group, the aim is to get back in touch with what has been temporarily lost; a contracted frontier. Members are helped to rediscover the thread of meaning and memory in their lives. In the ward group people can come and go as they please and sit at the periphery if they want. The members have had long psychiatric careers; the group provides support and enhanced human contact which the members can take at their own pace. This is a frontier worth working on. In an analytic group, however, they would find it hard to sit still, listen, interact and to be there for others.

The understanding and management of all groups can be enhanced by thinking along group-analytic lines but groups need to be designed or members sent to groups which fit their particular personal frontiers and preoccupying concerns.

The conductor is also a member of the group and must consider her own values, abilities and limitations. Perhaps she should not accept a person she dislikes strongly – the **negative placement** – in the hope that the group will sort him out. Probably the same goes for people she likes too much whom she may want to rescue, while not addressing important issues for fear of disturbing their relationship. Ideally, the conductor should have a basically positive feeling for each member. Misgivings could usefully be discussed with a colleague or in supervision. We cannot be all things to all men and it is important to recognise those people with whom we cannot work. Foulkes himself encouraged the use of the conductor's own personal reactions: 'This is only fair. After all, he is not making a selection for an abstract "group therapy", but for this group as conducted by him.' It is important to say no to such patients, to those to whom no help can be offered and to those for whom another form of therapy is indicated.

Group composition

Suitability for group therapy involves thinking about the *composition* of the group; not just who to have in the group, but who to have in with whom. Someone may be highly suitable for group therapy but not for *this particular group* (including the conductor). The blending involves balancing similarities and differences between prospective group members to create a *social microcosm*. These are concerns in all groups.

For *similarities*, the main guide is the 'Noah's Ark principle' (two by two) to avoid someone being the odd one out at risk of being scapegoated; the *only* black, or gay, or old, or young person there. There may be both a lack of support and empathy when no one has had similar experiences and the possibility of using this position to fend off genuine feedback: 'You're only saying that because I'm gay', could lead to escalation or stalemate without another gay man's point of view. The difficulty with having only two members of a particular grouping is that they may feel obliged to support each other even when they do not want to. The conductor must therefore remain aware of tensions that may arise between any pairs she has chosen. Moreover, applying this rigidly might lead to excluding someone from a group who is an isolate on one dimension but would otherwise use the group.

The conductor is also looking for *differences* so that interpersonal learning can take place. Foulkes preferred variety, including extremes, in which the one manifestly displays or personifies the potential of the other. Samuels (1964) suggested selecting people on the basis of what they can offer to each other and to the group. He argues that we should balance several factors including passivity, aggressivity, transference and ability to express affect. So three rather passive withdrawn people could be leavened with verbal aggressive people who can learn from each other. Or, in terms of transference, some anti-authoritarian members need balancing with some mediating ones to avoid a stuck group. Whitaker (1985) also says it is important to consider the preferred *mode* of expressing feelings. A group needs to have a *blend* of people who are at ease with expressing anger and sympathy. She talks of mixing people in terms of their preferred defences. These ideas should be borne in mind, although the reality of who is available may make balancing difficult and compromise necessary. Table 3.1 shows a typical selection of people who may be considered for group membership.

It is helpful to think about how one person's needs and patterns of relating may be similar to a second person's but reciprocal to a third person's. You cannot predict the whole – how your group will go – from the sum of its parts. However, you can select the members to create opportunities for having things in common *and* opportunities for learning new things from each other. This will give members a better chance of experiencing the support and identifications that come from the similarities *and* the changes and challenges that come from the differences. This attention to detail minimises difficulties later on and increases the therapeutic potential of the group. You will never establish the perfect group, but growing a good-enough one takes time (maybe nine months from the initial idea to the first session).

Preparation

There is evidence that preparation for the group reduces the number of people who leave prematurely. New members who drop out are often casualties left with increasing fears about joining another group or becoming involved in close relationships. Unexpressed feelings of rivalry or conflict between members, a fear of excessive dependence, or a feeling of lack of attention may cause their departure. The conductor needs to be sensitive to the pressures on the new member.

The member who *discloses prematurely* may be using a manic defence in response to anxieties about developing trusting and intimate relationships with others, and is also at risk of dropping out. In a preparation-cum-assessment session the therapist can recognise the risks of early dropout and address it with the potential member. Both are fore-warned. The new member may be encouraged to contract for a specific number of sessions or agree to a minimum set period of notice, rather than yield to the temptation to abandon ship after a few meetings. Preparation may require a few sessions or even some time in individual therapy. It can alleviate fears – for example, thinking that he will be the only nervous person at the first meeting – and clarify some misconceptions gained about group therapy from films or television. The potential group member is told that the group might seem strange, anxiety provoking and not obviously rewarding at first. A rationale is provided suggesting that if many of our problems are learned in groups, then the

Table 3.1 **Assessing and selecting for a group**

Name	Age	Sex	Marital status	Occupation	Education	Social and family background	Presentation	Main symptoms or problems	Previous treatment
A	42	M	S	Dental technician	Technical training	Father died when 'A' was 12, mother mentally ill. Irish Catholic	Depression	Social withdrawal, sexual abuse	Two years' individual therapy
B	38	F	M	Office work and artist	HNC	Mother psychotic illness, father bombastic and controlling. One sister, no children	Chronic unease and discontent	Intermittent paranoid feelings, inability to trust or find satisfaction	In-patient psychotic illness following end of first marriage; long-term psychiatric follow-up.
C	34	M	S	Salesman (unemployed)	'A' Levels	Only child, father not known. Lived in same house since age of 2.	Anxiety, depression, grief reaction	Anxiety and inability to work since learnt mother dying	None
D	29	M	M	Unemployed	Graduate	Eldest of three sons. Drank heavily. Aged 21 when mother died. Married with one young child.	Depression and alcoholism	Once trained, now unable to work. Marital problems	Community alcohol team Counselling Anti-depressants
E	74	F	W	Housewife	Degree in later life	Father died when 'E' was 10, youngest of eight children. Emigrated to Britain. Jewish.	Depression	Recurrent mood swings	ECT Lithium Counselling

group may be a good place to tackle them. This builds hope and trust in the process. The patient begins to find that he can help himself and allow others to help him, by being as open as he can (at his own pace) about his thoughts and feelings concerning his relationships – including those with other group members. He is invited to question the purpose of therapy and to raise any doubts. It is useful both to anticipate common problems in a hand-out and to encourage each individual to anticipate his personal difficulties; the conductor must see if these can be diminished by preparation-cum-assessment, or if they appear too much for the person to cope with in a group. During preparation, the prospective group member and the conductor establish a therapeutic relationship.

Some therapists think preparation spoils the development of transference but we agree with Yalom (1995) that transference is a fairly hardy plant that will grow anywhere. There is enough to be anxious about in joining a group without adding the anxiety of entering a totally unfamiliar environment. Preparation aims to keep anxiety to an optimal level for joining the group while allowing the prospective patient to make an informed decision about whether he wants to do so.

The Conductor

Co-therapy

Ideally where there are co-conductors, both will be involved from the beginning (although this does not always happen). If the conductor is going to have a co-therapist, her choice of partner is important. Many of the considerations involved in selecting group members will also apply in choosing a co-conductor. It is important to be clear about what the relationship will be. Time should be given to discussion of the co-conducting relationship and the meaning of any strong feelings between them which may reflect what is happening in the group, and are part of understanding the transference and countertransference within the group. (For a fuller discussion see Chapter 9.)

Choosing the group conductor

As well as asking if prospective members are suitable for the group, conductors should also ask if *they themselves* are suitable for this group. Although human beings are probably more similar than otherwise, the issues of race, culture, class and gender confound our attempts to communicate our shared experience of being human – indeed the list of issues is endless. The conductor should be mindful of her *position* in society (as a white, educated, middle-class woman, for example) being aware both of the values she brings to the group and of the way she may be experienced by the group as representing those values. Just as members are prepared for entry into a group, so too the conductor may need to be prepared in the ways and expectations of group members who come from different backgrounds to her own. This is particularly important for a homogeneous group where all members share an experience the conductor may not herself have had. So what of a man working with women survivors of sexual abuse (see Mann, 1989)? Or an Afro-Caribbean conductor in a group of Somalis?

There may also be particular aspects of a prospective conductor's personality or history which mean that she is not the right person to conduct a certain group. However, being anxious is not in itself a counter-indication.

The conductor's own anxieties: preparation for the conductor

'Trainees who are not anxious must be sick', wrote Berger *et al.* (1958) on the training of group psychotherapists. The conductor has selected, composed and set the group up, as we have described, and is starting to worry as the first session looms. What if she has forgotten something important? Suppose nobody turns up? Suppose they do, but leave after half an hour, or perhaps stay for the first session then never come back? It could become completely uncontrollable. They might even gang up on her! Or maybe there will be an hour and a half of silence. In reality, she may have forgotten something; not everything will go as planned; but the other things are highly unlikely to happen, except in her anxious dreams.

If the conductor has had to struggle against the organisational odds to start the group, she fears losing face and also letting down the cause of group therapy if something goes wrong (and she knows just who, in the organisation, will say 'I told you so!'). There will be eight other people sitting in a circle with her (if they all come) and subjecting her to genuine scrutiny as well as seeing her through the prism of transference. Additionally, each member will have been referred by someone. It is becoming a cast of thousands. Individual therapy has never seemed more attractive.

She may have become a victim of her own publicity, setting up within herself an unattainable image of the ideal therapist. Not being a perfect therapist does not mean public shame as, in reality, all she has to be is 'good enough'. Some people might rejoice at one of her group members acting out in a session or acting up on the way out ('You see, groups just make people worse'). The conductor needs to keep in touch with a community of thought which privileges open communication and the mobilisation of strong feeling when the organisational mores of her workplace contradict this. In the early stages she needs people to talk to for support, for rehearsing theory and for supervision (see Chapter 9, on training). If her own experience as a group member has been positive this will help her to sustain realistic expectations.

Gradually, the various elements of training are internalised and the therapist has more courage in her convictions, more faith in the process of therapy. Attention to structure, however, is a constant at any point along the learning curve of developing as a therapist. Experienced and less experienced therapists alike constantly contend with a cast, if not of thousands, of considerably more people than those actually in the room. There will always be some who are hostile, meddlesome or envious. They can threaten to spoil the group. These worries are not restricted to the new therapist. Talking about their causes may not dispel them, but it helps to know that difficult behaviour can be understood and worked with.

It is not the conductor's fears that cause problems, but the *defences she uses to deal with them*. Williams (1966) describes such defences as 'security operations' whereby new group therapists adopt special pseudotherapist roles to fend off personal threat. Supervision can help to ease a conductor out of her pseudotherapist role, an anxious dyadic relationship to the group as an entity, by deepening her understanding of the group as a whole ('including the conductor') and its dynamics. This is a long-term training issue, but a lot can be done to derail the development of anti-therapeutic security operations at the outset if the appropriateness of the therapist's anxieties is acknowledged.

Yalom (1995) describes common 'problems of neophyte group therapists'. These are:

1. experiencing the disorientating effects of group pressure
2. having people drop out, or forming subgroups, and fearing the end of the group is nigh
3. not tolerating being in the wrong or looking a fool
4. simple lack of familiarity with the phases of group development and maturation.

Often the neophyte therapist feels so ashamed of what she fears is happening in her group that she hides it, denying herself reassurance, support and the possibility of thinking about the situation afresh. In regretting her lack of power to make the group members do the things she wants them to, she may deny her power to decide how she behaves in the group. She must use this power to serve the therapeutic task of the group rather than her understandable need for security.

The new therapist cannot be blamed for her lack of knowledge or experience; she looks for a theoretical frame to help her make sense of her feelings and anxieties. She recognises that some of her anxieties may be part of her countertransference to the new group members who are also anticipating the start of the group with trepidation. She records her group and seeks supervision. She wants to run her first group with a more experienced co-conductor. She joins a group herself or finds one to observe. She looks for people who talk the same language. All this is her acting responsibly, and will be looked at in more depth in Chapter 9.

Starting Out: A Summary

Nitsun (1989) draws convincing parallels between the dynamics of early group formation and those of early development in infancy. In the first few months the group, like the infant, is struggling to achieve a sense of integration. At the start the group is not a unit, it is an unintegrated collection of individuals. They may experience anxieties associated with earlier periods of their own development when their very survival was at issue. The conductor is in an analogous position to the infant's caregiver, with the same function – that of holding. Nitsun (1989, p. 253) writes:

> Following the analogy, it is probably more important for the conductor to be there in a tangible way to help the group to feel safe, to define boundary issues clearly – all reflecting sensitivity to the anxieties and confusions of early group formation – than to maintain a position of determined therapeutic detachment or to make penetrating interpretations.

Dynamic administration functions like the holding and facilitating environment of early infancy (Winnicott, 1971). The conductor has done her best to protect the group structure from outside threats. In the room, she is now doing her best to contain group anxieties.

The group needs a 'good-enough' environment to overcome anxieties about survival, and become a living entity. Perfection is not required or possible. The things the conductor has to consider when growing a group are not rules. The group environment cannot be like the conditions of a scientific experiment or the asepsis of an operating theatre; it is bound to be human and messy. Things can be more complicated for the group, including the conductor, if she rushes through organising the group in a hurry to get on with the more exciting tasks of therapeutic activity. The conductor who gambles by including a particular member, or settles for a room next to a gurgling boiler, has accepted responsibility for the kind of group she is creating. She has not broken any rules, but her decisions have consequences for the group:

> The negotiations related to patient participation in an analytic group are... more numerous, difficult, and time-consuming than those required for individual treatment. (Mullan and Rosenbaum, 1978)

The trainee wishes 'this stuff' was all over and she could do some therapy. But it is better to realise its importance some time before finding oneself halfway up a drainpipe.

LEARNING POINTS

- The conductor draws a line around the group and sets its **boundaries**. This is done before the conductor even begins to meet with prospective group members.
- Her **dynamic administration** around these boundaries promotes the important holding function of any group she uses to help people.
- Setting up a group means working with the **setting** of the group. The conductor needs to establish a working relationship between herself, her group and the organisation which she is working in.
- The conductor does her best to ensure that the anxieties of being in a group (**internal space**) are not fuelled by what is going on around it (**external space**).
- Selection can be thought of in terms of this person's suitability for this group (and vice versa), that is, will he be able to *use* it?
- Group balance is a therapeutic technique. The attention the conductor gives to the composition of the group will enhance its therapeutic potential.
- 'Trainees who are not anxious must be sick.' A new group conductor needs to be able to recognise, acknowledge and work with her own anxieties.

■ Group therapy is a complicated business. We make it less complicated by attending to the details of growing a group, the setting and
dynamic administration.

■ Neither the conductor nor the group can be perfect. The conductor
tries to develop and maintain a 'good-enough' group.

■ There are no absolute rules for growing a group, only consequences
which have to be worked with (as we will see in Chapter 4).

WHAT HAPPENS IN A GROUP?

The development of the group: illustrated with an account of the life of one group

Introduction

We move from the perspective of the person joining and the conductor starting a group to take a bird's eye view of a group on a training course. We observe the group developing as the members of the group and the conductor interact, facilitating (or holding back) the group's effectiveness. We want to convey the particular quality of being in a group without describing an individual's experience; this is left to your imagination. As the narrative of the group members' interaction proceeds, we hear the accompanying internal monologue of the group conductor as he[*] strives to understand the process and decide upon his interventions. This provides a model of the conductor reflecting on the group interactions, his own countertransference and his knowledge of group theory, showing how much of his work is invisible. (The clinical material is distinguished from the conductor's reflections.)

The choice of a time-limited group enables us to illustrate the passage of the group from its beginning tasks, as it develops through its conflictual period into a mature group and on to its pre-determined ending. Research on group development, from different theoretical perspectives, suggests groups have persistent patterns, which Tuckman (1965) described as **forming, storming, norming** and **performing**. Rather than talking about phases of development (which may suggest a rigid view of phases moved through and not revisited) we prefer to think about the group having certain developmental tasks, which must be addressed if the group is to function effectively and will usually be revisited many times in the group's life.

---

[*]   In the rest of the book references to the conductor are to *she* but in this chapter we are writing about a particular male conductor and *he* is used.

Although the conductor attempts to observe the group and not impose a theoretical view, the choice of what is noted must be informed by theoretical assumptions. Each descriptive section is followed by some learning points and theoretical formulations which should both illuminate the clinical material and allow connections to be made to other groups, be they brief cognitive-behavioural groups, social skills groups, creative therapy groups or open-ended analytically orientated groups. Theoretical terms appear in bold type.

What to look for in this chapter

■ What signs can you find of the group changing?
■ How do you think it would feel to be a member of this group at different phases?
■ Can you see opposing forces being expressed in the group?
■ Can you see any subgroups forming?
■ What can you see the conductor doing which seems to have an impact on the group?
■ When does the conductor ignore individuals in the group's interest?
■ When does the conductor protect an individual?
■ What sort of strategies or interventions does he use?

Clinical Presentation

Initial phase of the group's development (forming)

Introduction

Although the conductor has not selected each patient as he might have done in an out-patient therapy group, but has arranged the distribution of students within the various groups with his colleagues, he sees himself as establishing the membership of the group and being responsible for the setting. As part of a course, the group meets in a room used for teaching with posters on the walls about drug addiction and AIDS. The room is away from the main building where the remainder of the programme occurs and other groups meet. This has implications which emerge in the first session. The importance of **dynamic administration** and the conductor's responsibility for its effects in establishing the group's **boundaries** is revealed in the beginning phase of this group.

In the first four sessions the individuals strive to become members of the group, creating ways of working together thus establishing some group cohesion within the group's boundaries. In group-analytic terms this is described as developing a group **matrix** or network of communication within which group members can feel *held*. They wonder how to use the group conductor to help them in this task. They tussle over who will have control and who will be close to whom. In this phase, two individual group members are prominent: Kingston deals with anxiety in the early part of the group by putting himself centre stage and the group conductor tries to protect him from suffering the consequences of his actions; Valerie wants to move from the city to a country idyll and the story of this move becomes an important metaphor in the life of the group.

> The conductor arrived, rather breathless, pulling in another chair, to the first session of a group that had suddenly gained a new member. The conductor said a few words about the aim of the group, which was followed by a hushed silence until the members started to introduce themselves. One person declined to give their name. Another commented: 'This group is rather large: perhaps too large.'

There was obvious unease at the size of the group, or perhaps the extra member and the conductor breaking the boundary. A group might be expected to address issues about confidentiality in a first session, but the emotional charge which is attached to it in this group (with one person not even being prepared to reveal their name) is probably reinforced by the conductor's approach to dynamic administration. By setting up the room for one fewer person than would actually be attending the group and pulling in a chair at the last minute he may have conveyed to the group some sense of hasty planning and uncertainty about who will actually be in the group and whether each individual member is valued. In Chapter 2 we described the way in which a baby needs maternal **holding** to protect him from intrusions into his world which he has not yet developed the capacity to respond to, and referred to such intrusions as **impingements**. Similarly this conductor has not succeeded in protecting his fledgling from impingements which it cannot cope with at this early stage. Conductors (like mothers) cannot always establish the ideal environment, but must be aware of and be prepared to address the implications of their actions.

Kingston began to question how the group would function. Would confidentiality be observed? Would power be respected or abused? How dangerous is the conductor? As if in response to unease at this discussion two members, who had previously sung in a choir together, recognised each other. It seemed reassuring to have something in common with someone else. 'It feels very lonely in the group', said one group member expressing people's need for contact. The self-designated couple looked at the floor and not at each other.

Anxiety appeared to be reduced as some of the fears were expressed and two people apparently reassuringly acknowledged their previous meeting. Yet there was still concern about whether the conductor would create a safe group, and what the implications might be of two people knowing each other in a group which was intended to be composed of strangers.

Kingston returned to talking about confidentiality, knowing that he was expressing his need to trust others. His demands for reassurance began to irritate the group.

Kingston is at risk of being **scapegoated** because he is the only group member who shows how anxious he is about how he will be treated. The implication is that the others do not need rules to make the group safe. Individuals often find themselves being drawn into enacting a particular **role** or function on behalf of the group. He is sucked into the role of *central person* (Redl, 1966) because the group is afraid to address the issue directly or to engage with the group conductor. The underlying process must be exposed to prevent the person who is being scapegoated being separated out from the group and even leaving prematurely. Here the conductor recognises the need to act firmly and assumes Kingston is expressing these fears for others; that they also worry about how the group will react to them if they speak personally. He is also showing the group how any individual communication within the group may be heard as having meaning for all the group members.

The conductor talks to the whole group, through his comment to Kingston. 'Kingston hopes the group will respect him if he explores the aspects of himself he does not respect.' Kingston agrees and there is a change of focus in the group. They are less irritated with Kingston and the tension is reduced.

Kingston has been noticed and appears to have felt understood by the conductor.

The group talks of how sitting opposite the conductor, like Kingston, is to be in the spotlight, but sitting next to him can seem to be in the silent, nameless shadow.

The ambivalence over the wish to be in Kingston's position, in the spotlight, special, but exposed, emerges. The shadow refers to the hidden aspects of the person. The other group members' irritation with Kingston may be their way of expressing anxiety at the possibility of addressing the hidden part of themselves, the unconscious, in the group. Their anxiety may be increased because of the ill-defined group boundaries. The group members must be wondering if the conductor will continue to break his own rules. He was unclear about the number of group members in his group, adding another one at the last minute, and now he has two group members who know each other when the group should consist of strangers. For the professionals, who are members of the group, the idea that they might know other group members in their daily life compromises their belief in the group as a free zone where they can explore themselves personally. As a new group they are struggling to deal with the anxieties that this failure has generated.

But there is a powerful attraction at being in the group spotlight which counterbalances the members' fears about the lack of safety in the group.

A woman confesses that she accidentally exposed someone at work and confidentiality was not maintained. She is shocked by what happened, and ashamed. She wants the group to accept her despite her vulnerabilities. Other mistakes emerge; someone has been censured at work for not being politically correct. A shock wave sweeps the group. Is the group going to expose the dark side of its members, the shadow?

The conductor is aware of the increasing sense of drama as this first group session draws to a close. The group members have seen from the beginning that his authority is imperfectly exercised. At this stage many group members' **transference** to the conductor may represent their feelings towards former carers who have let them down. The conductor wonders if his own feeling of failure may be understood as a **counter-transferential** response, which can illuminate the hidden meaning of the interactions between the group members.

The conductor's countertransference indicates that the group members are already making emotional connections between the experience of his unreliability in this first group and their own previous life experiences of receiving negligent care. Most of the group members hide from the recognition that the conductor has let them down by focusing on their own mistakes and failings. They attack Kingston as the one group member who is prepared to admit his anxieties and thus reveal their fears too. Trust is not developing; rather, the group is becoming frightened, defensively insisting that what is said in the group must be politically correct. Adopting such external rules masks overt attacks on the most vulnerable or the most powerful, and attempts to control the expression of the unacceptable aspects of human nature within the group. The group has chosen, temporarily, to reduce the tensions by *restricting* free and open communication. This is a **restrictive solution** (see Chapter 6) resolving the group's fears and anxieties. It does not support the wish to trust each other and establish their own rules and structures.

He comments that despite the group apparently addressing embarrassing issues there is a wish to not get down to the 'nitty gritty', and rules of correct social discourse will be used to censure what emerges.

The second session opens with a previously silent member saying the group was more interesting than expected. Another is surprised at having spoken. There is a need for more guidance. Silence reigns, until the difficulty of starting the group is likened to the difficulty of starting a car that has stalled. Is it the conductor's responsibility to get it started again? Perhaps it is flooded? The group does not pick up on the image.

It is difficult to express oneself clearly when more than one or two people are present. Kingston again talks of his insecurity in the group. Last week he felt ignored and got at, but he still wants to explore himself, in the group on his own.

Kingston again puts himself in line to become the group scapegoat although indirectly he is raising the question of how you use the group for all of its members.

Can one make bonds in the group? What is possible? What are the implications? Perhaps there is a need for a colleague for support? The conductor's comments are felt as demands to which one must respond and conform.

At the end of the second meeting the two key issues, of how you become a member of the group, and what is the role of the conductor, have become public; the group is starting to have a sense of itself.

There is a wish for guidance, members feel helpless, unable to act for themselves. Anger and perhaps disdain are emerging. One member feels the conductor is demanding obedience, requiring them to behave in a specified way.

Laughter ceases and the group falls silent as the conductor enters the third session. The involvement in the group is apparent as one member describes how much she has thought about what happened in the group. Another member wants to know that the others recognise the risks he has taken in the group. While one woman is preoccupied with her situation at work another fears she will miss out through her absence at the next session. Helen tells a dream about the group in which she is choosing whether to be in or out of the group.

The conductor's entry marks the group's boundary, pinpointing a move from ordinary chit-chat into the group's own tensions and anxieties. The silence affirms the growing sense of the group's shared preoccupations (**group cohesion**) and the conductor's special role within the group process.

In individual psychotherapy a dream is seen as having unconscious meaning for the dreamer and the dreamer's transference to the psychotherapist. In a group, Foulkes (1964, p. 127) suggested that: 'Every dream told... is the property of the group.' In this case the connection is explicit but even when a dream seems much more individually based the conductor needs to hold onto Foulkes' maxim. A dream may also be used defensively to resist the group process and make a bid for individual attention. Like the earlier example of the scapegoat, we begin to see how events in the group are understood in terms of their meaning for the dynamic of the whole group. Yet the conductor knows that an intervention or silence may have particular significance for an individual member. Here the dream continues to give rise to group associations.

Doubts about being in the group emerge as someone talks of the conductor not valuing members' comments.

As always, opposite emotions are present in a group. Following the expression of positive feelings, the dream heralds the doubts.

Is the conductor Puck in Shakespeare's A Midsummer Night's Dream? Playful ideas emerge. There are thoughts of taking the conductor's chair but there is also a fear of expressing anger. The conductor is likened to the Buddha. 'If you meet the Buddha on the road, kill him', is the response.

In the third session members begin to work together to explore their dependence on the conductor and their frustration with his inadequate responses; in spite of one group member feeling that the conductor demands conformity, the group is able both to explore more personal responses and to develop the dream about group membership into a series of more imaginative associations culminating in the fantasy that they could get rid of the conductor (killing the Buddha). They are on the edge of some crucial developments, have risked attacking the conductor and are left wondering if this is acceptable. They have also expressed their need for intimacy.

Frustration and exasperation with an initial silence in session four results in the conductor being likened to a school teacher. Valerie talks of her wish to move to the country. How can she negotiate leaving a lively city centre with her family? The conductor tries to support free association between the group members and appears to ignore the dilemma which Valerie would like the group to help her with.

The conductor also has a dilemma: by ignoring Valerie's problem he is trying to educate and shape the group, conveying that to focus on Valerie's problem, as if it could be solved by questioning and advice, will neither help Valerie nor address the issues which beset the group – namely how to relate to each other and whether they can challenge the conductor's authority. Yet by not taking up Valerie's dilemma he could be seen as opting out and behaving like Valerie's partner. 'But that's all one can expect from a facilitator.' Pauline and Simon both feel personally engaged at this point in the group.

There is an excited discussion about how you can find a bolthole in the tranquil country at the same time as entering a relationship. Can you be free to be close or distant to your partner and the bustling city at will? Pauline is angry at the discussion of Valerie's move, hijacking her agenda. Simon describes a very different experience from an idyllic pastoral life. For him home is the trauma of being wedged between a religious maniac and a couple caught up in a *folie à deux*.

As session four starts the group has a dilemma; can the conductor survive further attack? Gaining no clues from the conductor, the group responds to its dilemma through a solution offered by Valerie. Discussing Valerie's house move, an outside situation, takes the anxiety away from the group. She needs a bolthole to escape from the city and pressure of strange people (as Kingston expressed in the first session), but in her plan to move into the country this need will disappear. Moving will create beautiful, harmonious, sensual relationships. Allowing a woman to take authority for the group also resolves the authority issues with the male conductor. Indirectly, using the metaphor of Valerie's move to the country and her assumption of the role of temporary leader in the group, the group continues to work on its dilemma.

Two subgroups form, with the men a little wary about Valerie's taking so much control in the family. They behave much like Valerie's partner at home, and the conductor in the group, leaving her to drive the agenda. There is a feeling of helplessness, being controlled by crazy forces, by religious fervour (perhaps an expression of group dependency), and the madness of a totally involved relationship, in the *folie à deux*. For the moment the group needs this solution of Valerie moving where she wishes to hold it together: although it means disowning intense frustrations and not addressing their disappointment with the conductor as leader. They trust each other and there is a temporary lull before the storm.

By the end of the fourth session, the initial phase of group development has taken place and group cohesion is growing. Two issues emerge: who will have control or be controlled, and who will be close to whom? Members struggle with the conflict between their desire to depend on the conductor, wishing him to provide guidance and leadership, and their frustration when he does not appear to attend to individual needs. While some are able to confront him, one person has to conform to what the conductor wants (being in the grip of her transference to him as a significant figure from her past). At this stage in the group's development the conductor chooses not to interpret her transference but to focus on the conflicts over how to relate to him and to each other.

Review of initial phase of group development

Theoretical discussion and learning points

The conductor's training in psychotherapy makes him aware of how his own personality and theoretical biases influence the content of the group. The aim is to be aware of these influences rather than trying to eliminate them. The conductor sees the group struggling to develop a matrix which allows the members to integrate the past with present experience both in and outside the group. Although he is aware that past experiences influence individuals' contributions to the group, at this stage he focuses on the experience *in* the group. When one theme or feeling emerges, a counter theme or force comes to the fore as the group attempts to establish a balance. How these forces are used or avoided by the group will shape its future development.

Drawing on the work of Bennis and Shepherd (1956), the conductor hypothesises that there are two fundamental issues which all individuals face with ambivalence: authority and intimacy. How dependent or independent should the individual be? How close to others or distant from them should one become? In the early group the members struggle to address these questions by enacting the polarisations between the opposing forces, and thus develop a restrictive solution. By commenting on the group's fears of getting down to the nitty gritty and their use of social censure, he hopes to facilitate another solution emerging in which acknowledging the difficulties of plain speaking will increase the range of thoughts and feelings. Similarly when Valerie and the group focus on her desire to move to the country he attempts to return the group to its own problems. This time he is unsuccessful but they do work on their own issues through the medium of Valerie's problem.

LEARNING POINTS

■ **Dynamic administration**
The group conductor takes full responsibility for the setting of the group, for the selection of the members and for the boundary setting in the group. If things go wrong (even if something happens which is not really the conductor's 'fault') the conductor must acknowledge responsibility so that the group can examine the impact the mishap has on the group's process. The same is true in a structured group. Even though the group will probably not explicitly discuss boundary issues, the conductor will need to be aware of the impact they have.

■ **Group development**
All groups have similar patterns of development. Personal and group development can only occur if there is conflict within the group. The conductor should expect this and not misunderstand the personal attacks. At this early stage the conductor limits the destructive attempts to solve these conflicts through dependency (often an overdependency either on the conductor or on a selected group member or subgroup), scapegoating or flight from the group.

■ **Becoming a member of the group**
The initial challenge to each person is to become a member of the group. More structured groups offer an induction which can allay the

inevitable anxieties of working out how to relate to others. Exposing these anxieties (as happens in this group example) has the therapeutic potential of revealing recurrent patterns of behaviour which individuals use to feel in control in a group where they are observed and, eventually, challenged. Frustrated with the conductor's apparent lack of guidance, members join a temporary subgroup, challenging the conductor's authority and working out how to operate more effectively in the group as each one comes to feel more a part of the group.

■ **Developing group cohesion**
In this early phase group cohesion develops as the members and the conductor jostle among themselves trying to find out how they can work together. The group may need to weather a challenge to an idealised unified state recognising that cohesion involves accepting and respecting differences too.

Challenging the structure of the group (storming)

The conductor tells the group its physical location will move! Following the previous week's discussion on moving, there is disbelief. Anger at the move turns into frustration at the endless discussion on moving houses the previous week. The group is angry with Valerie. The conductor questions this. Talk moves to reports of jobs changing or disappearing. One person wants to take flight from the group. The conductor tried to draw their attention back into the group and to their feelings about the new venue which would once again disrupt their continuity. Group members wanted to ignore the more immediate shared subject matter of their feelings about the group and the conductor and to discuss external matters. They tried to deal with their anxiety by avoiding this more intimate topic and concentrating on outside matters. It seemed as if this sudden upheaval had destroyed any hope of this family hanging together through the move. The conductor, challenging this restrictive solution, brought the group to life, with them feeling 'pushed around'.

The conductor had delayed telling them about the change of venue until they had developed sufficiently to be able to address the issues that might arise. He knew that a change of physical location would disturb any group and particularly this one which had started with some wobbly boundaries. He has to take responsibility for the move since the group cannot resolve its feelings towards an anonymous authority and learn from the experience. Even so, initial anger with the conductor is displaced onto the scapegoat, Valerie, because of her position as the group spokesperson through her activity in the previous session.

Bion (1961) (whose accounts of different ways of escaping from the group task is given in Chapter 8) described this mode of group evasion as **fight or flight**. The conductor recognises that both the attack on Valerie and the desire to take flight from the group indicate their need for the conductor to contain them. He helps them to focus on their immediate feelings rather than allowing them to settle for an easy escape route. This gives them the confidence to express their feelings about this change and what it evokes.

Anxiety emerged, as in the first session, people fearing they would get lost, unable to find the new location. Future absences were reported, members clearly questioning their commitment to the group. Kingston, as in the first session, plays a central role wanting the group to move on and not allow upsets to interfere with the group's exploring relationships. Speaking for the group, Kingston cautiously presses others to be involved, while they seem to be actively withdrawing. But Kingston, as before, was not really exploring his relationships with the others, but wanted to explore aspects of himself. The conductor presumed Kingston was also expressing some of the ambivalence of the group: avoiding intimacy, while wanting it, and comments that 'Kingston fears being penetrated by the group.' Pauline is outraged at this remark, and talks of a total loss of security in the group.

The group appears to regress to its original state of confusion and uncertainty, and Kingston takes a central role in an insecure situation when there is anxiety about belonging and being involved. He wants the group to carry on looking at him and his problems. Kingston again responds to the group's recurrent uncertainty by offering himself as a focus and scapegoat, as has possibly occurred in his past. The conductor hopes a personal interpretation to Kingston will also address some of the group's difficulties about maintaining intimacy in this newly threatening situation. On reflection the conductor wonders why he made this interpretation and what effect it might have had on the long-term development of the group's cohesion. He is aware that the group's anxieties may be **projected** onto him, making it harder for him to be the containing conductor the group needs. Instead of tolerating and acknowledging the group's frustration he may have been acting it out by *attacking* Kingston with his interpretation possibly repeating the kind of interaction which Kingston experienced in the past. Is the conductor expressing his own fear of being penetrated by the disturbance in the group? Despite understanding the group's response the conductor is caught up in the process and is unable to facilitate and interpret it.

It is unclear what the outcome will be. Perhaps Pauline's outrage is an individual's feeling about what the conductor has done to the group by proposing the move. This energy could act as a force moving the group on to explore their involvement with each other.

The next session opened with Pauline's penetrating and dominating laugh. The move disturbed her. She wants to be in control. Kingston described how last week's group was threatening, then enlarged on his indecision as to whether he wants to be in or out of a relationship. The group wanted him to say what he had to say clearly. His statements were often confused, his speech reflecting his indecision.

The group challenges Kingston to be more clearly involved but attempts to keep the group focused on interactions between group members failed, and the group discussed becoming involved with distant people.

It seemed easier to be in love with someone who wasn't physically close. Some members preferred fantasies of relationships, while others thought about how things could have been. In this the sadness of how this group could have been is apparent. A poignant commentator wondered if all close relationships are essentially *folies à deux*.

A subgroup offering the solution of self-sufficiency led to some others, who perhaps wanted to be dependent, feeling rejected.

There is a lively interchange between members in this session, but the investment is in relationships outside the group, for the unobtainable. Pauline's discussion of relationships outside the group becomes a major focus to which the group repeatedly returns. Earlier she had been frustrated by having her agenda hijacked by Valerie. Now her outrage at exploring a wish to be intimately involved in the group is followed by her investment in a past friendship which never develops. There is sadness in the group at what is not occurring here, and their need to avoid interactions in the present.

The conductor presumed the discussion of outside relationships was a necessary defence to reduce tension in the group, enabling the group and the relationship with the conductor to continue by re-establishing some sort of secure boundary.

There were absences without explanation at the next session.

The absences suggested something inadequately contained the previous week, which the conductor thought might emerge symbolically in the session's content.

Early on there was an interchange between a woman and a man. He could have felt put down, but seemed fascinated by her. This was noted by others, and the two struggled to explore some of their similarities, but at this point in the group's development it was not possible.

The similarities could only become movingly apparent in a much later group.

A woman notices another's seductive posture. Different descriptions of ideal relationships with parents, antagonism to mothers, and how it may be better not to see parents for years, emerge. A lengthy discussion seems to replay the process by which a son left home for years. Although he appeared to be motivated by 'a worthy cause', really he was escaping from the powerful emotions his mother stirred up in him. At the end the group is potentially freed by a member's interpretation. She talks of wanting to make social contact but being afraid that closeness will lead to a fear of being hurt. Through expressing her own dilemma she pinpoints the dilemma confronting the whole group.

The conductor is less active and at the end a member makes the crucial interpretation about the group, torn between its desire for more intimacy and the fear of being hurt. This suggests that the group has worked through some of its initial resistance to facing the early feelings stirred up by the need to move location. The conductor was knocked off balance by the intensity of the projective identification in the first of these three sessions but since then through his self-analysis he has gained an understanding of the unconscious processes of the group. Now he can contain his own internal conflicts, he is able to support the group members in struggling with the challenge to the structure and boundaries of their group. He enables them to regain their capacity for involvement.

Review of challenging the structure of the group

Theoretical discussion and learning points

The conductor made the assumption that, based on his view of the importance of dynamic administration, moving the group's location would be a major emotional issue. Ideally the group should have a consistent location but if external circumstances prevent the conductor from achieving this he sees himself as responsible.

At this phase of the group's development the conductor is thinking about his own countertransference, distinguishing it from his transference to the group. He tries to differentiate emotions which are unconsciously projected into him through the process of **projective identification** by group members and his responses to the group which arise from his own personal issues. Thus he thinks about whether his interventions were a result of overwhelming anxieties projected onto him by the group or rather a result of his own strong feelings about the group material. He recognises that he has strong feelings about the material. He understands a wish to be potent as an identification with the men whom he feels are being undermined by the women. These sessions show clearly how both the conductor and the members are caught up in the group processes. This is part of what Foulkes (1975, p. 3) meant when he wrote about a group-analytic approach being therapy 'by the group, of the group, including its conductor'. He also reflects on the implications of his interventions and what he sees happening in the group. He wonders whether he was propelled into premature activity and focused on intimacy when the group was actually preoccupied with issues of power and authority stemming from his moving the group location.

One way of looking at the material is to recognise the group's preoccupation with relationships with parents and being pulled between them, in contrast with the relationship between the child and one parent. In the Oedipal situation issues of power are to the fore and the group needs clear boundaries.

Alternatively, focal conflict theory explains the way in which the group, fearful at continuing its pursuit of intimacy in the light of structural disruption, tries to resolve its dilemma by focusing on relationships which may promise intimacy but are outside the danger zone of the group.

LEARNING POINTS

■ **The conductor as boundary manager**
   The conductor has not been able to protect his group boundaries from intrusion by the management. Although it is not his fault that the group has to move he has to take responsibility so that the group can discover and express responses to this situation, recognising that he too feels involved.

■ **Using countertransference in the group**
   The conductor notes that the group, unable to process its own material, uses him as a vehicle for its own undigested projections. He

will try to distinguish between this and his own feelings and responses towards the group. Thinking about countertransference can be applied to all types of groups including social and community groups.

■ **Maintaining group cohesion under threat**
The group is able to digest the blow to their fragile structure and return to work on it. This has required the conductor to stay as firm as possible through using boundary management and countertransference to contain the group as it uses some temporary solutions. The group is able to tolerate the threat of moving location because a degree of group cohesion has been achieved.

■ **Tolerating uncertainty as part of the conductor's role**
Sometimes it is not possible to reassure the group that the conductor has facilitated development or to take up the position of wrongdoer. This uncertainty can be uncomfortable for the conductor, but is vital for the group's ongoing sense of security within which further exploration will be possible.

Middle Phase in Group Development

In session nine the conductor was seen as manipulative, or just plain insensitive, handing out papers describing the group's new location. The group's interaction suggests that there may be irritation with each other and the conductor but this is not expressed directly. The anger dissipated as the group listened to one member movingly describing a tragedy as she was pulled between her mother and father. Some became angry on her behalf, and the group was obviously shaken by her story. Should this person have chosen to stay with her father or mother? How does one respond to parents who row and one has to choose between them? In this session there was discussion of both the reliable father to turn to, and the idealised father who became weak. There was also talk of a missing person. Was someone or something missing in this group? Sadness at the approaching break was expressed.

The tragic consequences of unresolved Oedipal conflict, and of rivalry between men and women were apparent. Initially there were derogatory remarks about fathers and the men in the group which perhaps referred to the conductor as well. However the group continues to explore relationships between men and women and the difficulties in asserting one's own authority without destroying the possibility of intimate and affectionate relationships. Lewis became the spokesman for the men.

The group wondered if one man's absence in the session before the break was because he had been put down by a woman. As Lewis talked of feeling he and the men were attacked in the group the rivalry between the sexes became apparent. One member described the tension of work, but it would be exposing to consult the counsellor: anxieties of the first session remain. Another told of relatives dying, but when she became upset at work she was criticised by bosses who did not approve of any expression of emotion by staff. Where do we get support if we are put down?

A member commenting on the group process questioned why contributions were always presented as complete. Members realised that they rarely asked each other how something had developed or what had happened following the previous week. Becoming aware of the potential destructiveness of their hidden rivalry and competitiveness, they were able to show a new level of concern for one another.

The increasing support in the group led to further discussion of the irritation between the men and women. Lewis kept his head down, not wanting to be a bore, and wondering how to be acceptable here. Could he confront these women, and their unreasonable demands? If he responded to the women would he deal with his feelings about the conductor? To address the conductor and respond to the women is perhaps too much to expect of himself.

Again an individual's past comes alive in the present scenario of the group. Lewis lost his father early in life and was brought up by his mother. In a dyadic relationship he did not have to respond to a triadic Oedipal situation developmentally, and now has difficulty contemplating it.

Lewis described himself as the one in the group who wilts in the face of the demands of women and authority. This led to a further change as others described similar difficulties in addressing both the group members and the conductor.

People felt their loss at not having recognised the potential for affection within the group. Simultaneously they were angry as they realised it was not available in adequate measure. The anger and frustration people felt towards their rejecting mothers and their absent fathers was discussed. Comments were made about the conductor being distant and absent, dressed in his raincoat, impervious to anything thrown at him. Bosses were generally abusive!

A new physical location following the break

No one is lost. The new room is an improvement and less clinical, but the remainder of the building, where the course occurs, is criticised.

Is this evidence of **splitting**, and if so can it be seen as the group valuing and protecting itself?

Prior to the conductor entering the group the lighting was altered. Perhaps this was a way in which the group could take possession of the room. One member's mother with Alzheimer's disease has moved into a 'home' and tragically does not recognise her, only her brothers. Another describes how much she has given up to care for her sick father, and others talk of the unique qualities of their male partners.

Hope is rekindled for a containing, responsive and warm group home, but this brings up sad memories of the limitations of mothers, and how it seems it is only the men who are special, taking on a maternal role, as has the conductor, in creating the new home for the group. While Helen is used to distract the group, Joan later expresses the group's rage and disappointment.

It becomes progressively more difficult for the men to talk in this session. Helen describes liking a younger man at work, and considerable pressure is put on her by other women to establish a relationship with him. The conductor confronts this group flight to solve the difficulties of even talking with the men in this group by persuading Helen to have a relationship elsewhere.

The conductor is not questioning the appropriateness of Helen's having a relationship with this man, but the group's emotional investment in it. The group are projecting their conflict into her, pushing her to resolve it for them.

A dramatic shift occurs as the group begins talking of the difficulties of being close to fathers; this is graphically portrayed at the end of the session when the conductor points out that the group has run out of time as a man describes trying to talk to his father for six years; yet his father always brings someone else along, who gets in the way.

The conductor ends two more sessions similarly before interpreting how the status quo is maintained, the son not creating a proper opportunity or allowing time to talk with his father.

The hope of establishing a new rapport in the group is short lived as the conductor tells of his planned absence from a future session. Joan expresses her rage saying that if a man tries to take over she will go for the jugular. If the man was gay, then it would be different. She describes her father's sadistic pleasure in beating his naughty children in a somewhat ritualistic way. New difficulties now appear in the group voiced through a man's problems with his threatening female boss at work. The group listens carefully and empathically, but does not address the issue the following week.

How will it be without the conductor? The conductor can just go off, breaking the contract. There is discussion of mob rule. A dream is told of a person pleading with the conductor to stay and not make them redundant. The dream is seen as an omen that the conductor will have an accident and not return. A child's clinging to mother when left at play school is described. People speak about not fitting into this society and feeling the shame of not having enough money. Slowly members describe feeling ashamed of expressing their dependence on the conductor.

This was resolved through projection into a subgroup. 'It's the men in this group who express weakness.'

Should the group tell the conductor what had happened when he was away? Joan had clearly expressed her wish for him to stay. Then, despite her anger with men, she took the conductor's chair. Some saw this as a way of denying the conductor's absence while coping with Joan's delinquency and threat of violence. Others were unhappy with what they felt was a defensive position the group had taken. They all considered they functioned better in many ways without the conductor; how would they now reintegrate him? One member wished he would stay away, linking it to the mixed feelings it had brought up about her father.

The group talked of fathers who seemed absent for many members. Others talked of their fathers who are now dying, and the struggle to get close. For some, fathers had been key people, someone they were proud of. Could they value what they had from their fathers or only be angry for what they had not had? Were they glad the conductor was back, or just fed up with how his return had interfered with their effective functioning as a group? Later in the group the men started discussing how they had been influenced by their mothers' expectations.

While the action of the member in taking on the conductor's role can be understood at a personal level, as a response to an unresolved Oedipal conflict, where a masochistic identification with the sadistic father resulted in this woman being unable to individuate, she was also expressing the group's need to find a new way to be with this abusive and neglectful conductor.

Much changed in the session following the conductor's absence. Men appeared in the group as equals, and there was an integration of the male/female subgroups. There seemed to be a resolution of authority issues, and the potential of a new way of relating to both parents and the conductor. But the next group opened very differently.

'This group is not as alive as another group I was in, I want more confrontation.' This is seen as a personal attack by another who invites the speaker to sort out their disagreements. Helen feels put on the spot but slowly describes her envy of the other person.

The social veneer of the 'nice' group masks anger and frustration.

Images of controlling their anger emerge. One talks of a red hot lump, another links it to the conductor and her father. To speak in this group, say what you want, means you may 'be pushed over the edge'. Kingston doesn't want to go over the top, and talks of his fear of being angry, or is it potent? 'How can one share a bed with one's girlfriend in her parents' house, even though invited to do so by them?' Is there a fear of arousing envy and castration by her father? Further talk of worrying about intruding and pushing people occurs, or of members' point of view not being heard if they should speak, and their desire (to be special) not recognised.

Following the re-establishment of the group after the conductor's absence, issues about authority emerge with a new vigour. The power struggles arouse feelings of sadistic attack, excitement, fear and a need for security in the face of mob rule. The group manages to contain this and is left with a sense of power and energy which does not disappear, but needs to be addressed repeatedly. The group was not ready to have a rapprochement with the conductor and move on. Challenging a group structure excessively results in primitive regressive defences being used.

A new world?

Can the folie à deux end? The session returns to an earlier theme with the news that the houses are sold. They are free to move. Two members are moving. Has last week's session settled something? But there are hints of unfinished business. Perhaps there is still something unresolved?

Pauline's relationship has not developed and the group is disappointed. Some persuade her to try again. A voice comments: 'Everything seems to happen elsewhere, out of the group.' Lewis feels left out: he wants Pauline to talk with the men here. 'Yes, he does like her.' It's still difficult to believe things can be found in the group.

A heated exchange occurs about whether it is appropriate to discuss outside relationships in the group. Those less involved in outside events want more interaction in the group. Perhaps Pauline is expressing some feelings for the group. Others take this up, describing having used their energy to pass exams, write papers, do things on their own they thought their families wanted. But it doesn't lead to acceptance by parents.

With this realisation, there is a search for the men in the group, some of whom are absent. The women want more input from them. It then becomes apparent they do not exist as individuals. Do people only exist to meet others' needs? The men refuse to respond to the complaints about them. 'We won't be played with.'

The difficulties described in relationships outside the group now emerge in the group. The group is more alive when it focuses on what is happening within it; perhaps the tension can be resolved here. The conductor's persistence in linking outside events to the group has paid off and the group interacts far more independently.

LEARNING POINTS

■ **Developing interaction within the group**
The conductor consistently encourages the group to focus on what is happening in the room between themselves as the best way for the group members to learn and change. Individuals also need personal attention and issues outside the group are talked about. Both these activities can be resisted but sometimes enable the group to work symbolically.

■ **The conductor's absence**
An established group can usefully meet without the conductor and the change in power relations may allow things to emerge which the conductor's presence inhibits. It is important to prepare the group, ensuring that their responses to being left come to the surface. The conductor may be severely attacked for abandoning them for some other purpose.

Subgroups Emerge: The Transition to the Mature Group

One member felt supported by the conductor the previous week. The conductor suggests there is a need for a supportive father. As one person talks of her father, others describe being special in individual therapy, that has now ended. A man speaks of re-establishing his relationship with his father.

At the beginning of this session there is a rapprochement with the conductor. There is the potential for a valuable relationship with him.

It is opposed by others who describe how impossible fathers have been and continue to be. This leads to talk of competition with mothers, but no competition in the group is apparent and the women resolve to become a cohesive subgroup, of independent, uninvolved women who need neither fathers or mothers. 'The women are on top in this group.'

The women are subgrouping around stereotypical roles which deny difference and the potential for individuation. This acts as a defence against feelings aroused about creatively or supportively working together: and about the still secret subgroup from another meeting within the course.

Another subgroup emerges as Kingston wonders how involved he should be with his girlfriend. Some women join this subgroup, focusing around valuing personal relationships and talk of the loss of close friends. There is a warm exchange.

The stereotypical subgrouping is challenged by a personal statement. Addressing the need for intimacy challenges the idea of being independent and uninvolved and leads the group to explore their need for each other. The male/female subgroups dissolve, and subgrouping develops around the issue of whether people should be close or distant.

The integration of these two subgroups finally occurs through **mirroring**.

The increasing irritation between a man and a woman is commented on by others. Pushed by Kingston, Helen owns to being repulsed by him. It is the way he shows his neediness. She is suddenly shocked by the statement she has just made. The group contrasts the statement with the self-control she normally shows. The man is not put down by her attack, and happily owns to this aspect of himself. As she talks she realises she despises the neediness in herself, and begins to recognise the side of herself which has been split off and projected into this man.

During this moving exchange the group supports and helps both to speak. These two members are expressing and addressing issues relevant to all. They can now explore the relationship between the constantly emerging male and female, and the dependent and self-reliant subgroups.

There is a reduction of persecutory anxiety after this, and a desire for greater integration. Those who have spoken less personally are invited to say more. Differences are allowed as each member's specific needs are accepted. The new understanding of the group process does not mean that all the difficulties disappear. One person closes his eyes, another is pleased a break is coming. In response to the break some members invest themselves in groups elsewhere, but the group has developed enough to understand and respect these needs.

Review of the transitional phase of the group

Theoretical discussion

The ability to work through a stormy period leads to establishing ways of being together as a group and in subgroups while respecting each other's individuality.

The group works on its transference to the group conductor through discussing the difficulties they have in relating to their own fathers. The conductor's absence leads them to experience powerful and often primitive feelings which they are reassured to discover they can contain, neither repressing them nor being taken over by mob rule.

It is through defining the boundaries around the subgroups followed by their dissolution that the mature group emerges, once the group has achieved a rapprochement with the group conductor. The polarisation within the subgroups pushes group members to realise how they are different from their subgroup. The subgroups dissolve when the members of one realise that the other subgroup is a projection of what they deny in themselves. Foulkes termed this process of mutual self-recognition in groups mirroring.

LEARNING POINTS

■ **The importance of storming**
  All groups develop greater intimacy and honesty through knowing that the conductor and group members can accept and contain aggressive and destructive feelings. Otherwise the storm may be pushed into one person who becomes an outsider and leaves, or the group may remain a pallid place where no serious work can be done.
■ **The conductor's task is to survive**
  However uncomfortable, difficult or frightening it may be, the conductor has to accept the group's attacks, understanding their roots in the group members' own early experiences. Justifying

himself, because he feels guilty towards the group, will inhibit their expression of anger and disappointment leading to a false friendship between conductor and group.

■ **The role of subgrouping and mirroring**
Subgroups may seem to be a destructive way of polarising conflicts within a group but in discovering that one subgroup mirrors the other further integration may occur.

The Mature Group

The feelings of irritation and guilt that one member feels towards another appear to have kept the group alive, but not missed, over the break. The irritation is quickly addressed and the group moves on to looking at relationships here. One person got lost coming, others are pleased to be back. A member has a new job, and has sorted out problems with a female boss. The reintegration of the group is questioned as Valerie describes how unhappy her daughter is with the family's move. The conductor links the conflict out there to the feelings here as the group comes together after the break. The response to this comment is for the women and men to subgroup. But the subgroups rapidly reintegrate, and there is a wish for the men to become more involved with the women.

After the break, there is a rapid replay of the group's development, in which the group's defensive solutions re-emerge. The ambivalence at the closeness is possibly expressed the week after when the men are nearly all away. There is joking about this, but no linking to the previous week's events.

Valerie cautiously asks if she can talk about difficulties at home with her daughter. She pours her heart out, describing how her daughter is making life impossible with attacks on all the family members. She seems permanently angry, blaming her mother for the move, for taking her away from all her friends. She stays out late. Having had a fight with another girl, she has to travel across town on her own to her old school. The group responds to her distress with questions about what she has been allowed to do before, what controls have been applied, how involved is her father. Practical advice is offered. The whole group tries to empathise with her, but is ineffective and the demand for help with the problem continues.

The group is totally involved with helping and caring for their patient.

The conductor comments: 'We can have fantasies about Valerie's daughter which will be based on our experience, and then treat the mother and daughter relationship on the basis that our experience is the same as theirs, but we can't know what the daughter feels or how she is. What we can know are Valerie's feelings as they are at this time in this group.' Valerie then talks about how she feels, and links are made between the adolescent daughter and Valerie's adolescence. She fears her daughter will control her as her mother did. As Valerie expands on the awful relationship between her mother and herself, others resonate and share their feelings and difficulties with their mothers and with themselves as parents. A man wonders if women are always vicious? A sense of the 'life cycle' emerges as one woman talks of her father becoming a child again because of his illness, furious with her as he no longer has control over his situation and she will not do what he wants. Others share their experience of caring for their ageing parents.

The group develops a wish just to leave their families behind and go off on a powerful motorbike. Perhaps the bike owned by the one man in this session. But none of the women has a motorbike, only a push-bike which is either shut in the garden shed, or has been given away by the mother.

Moving the focus of the group from Valerie's experience in her external life to the experience of the members in the present stopped her being the group patient. Valerie's distress deserved recognition but it is not helpful to treat an outside relationship. Through focusing on her intrapsychic and interpersonal experience in the group, Valerie gains a new understanding of her distress, providing a different structure in which to contain her difficulties. The group can concentrate on its present experience and does not need to use outside events as a defence against conflicts it cannot face. (Contrast this with what happened in earlier sessions.) The group develops empathy with Valerie's experience. Others explore and confront their struggles as they resonate with her about mothers. The group comes alive with every member participating. Gender issues are explored playfully as the women consider using, if not owning, a motorbike. Confirmation of the importance of the absent men emerges in the following group.

Is it the pressures in the group, or a small operation, that made one man want time on his own? Another states he was determined to come this week in view of the challenge to him to be more involved. The difficulties of being in a relationship, especially if there are children, is raised by the men.

As the men return they begin to consider indirectly whether something happened in the group two weeks ago which had led them to miss the following group. They are beginning to explore for themselves how absences and boundary issues are an expression of the conflicts in the group.

Members become aware of the rapid approach of the end of the group. They are shocked by the sadism of one member who pierces slugs on knitting needles to protect the tender young shoots in her garden. Is the conductor the slug who is nibbling the growing point of the group away? The conductor's aggression in ending the group is diluted as the group is told needling slugs is no longer practised. There is a wish for the group to continue for another year.

There is a pause in the group, as if something needs to be said. Talk of the group ending makes Diana aware of what she has not done. She speaks of a person who has committed suicide: then how the conductor's absence aroused feelings... anxiety... upset... about her father. She now avoids contact with the conductor, who becomes drawn into a personal exchange with her. The group suggests she is expressing confused feelings others cannot yet put into words.

The group may be on the edge of a new level of exploration. Through the conductor's absence, yet ongoing presence, Diana recognises a split-off aspect of her self which she fears to address.

Will the group work with the intense confused emotions being expressed or stay with the more thought-out contributions? Joan expresses some of the difficult feelings aroused by the group ending.

The session opens with the group sympathising with the member whose father has died. Sadness is shared as members reflect on who they have lost and who may soon die. 'It's only now five years after my father died I realise how much I've lost!' The contrasting view is expressed by Joan who considers: 'Perhaps she can now be free and get on with her own life.'

The conductor wonders silently whether this an empathic response or a projection by Joan into the bereaved person.

The group, questioning her statement, starts to explore Joan's relationships. It slowly emerges she sees death leading to freedom but is herself unable to be free. Death seems the only way out of a relationship. Joan wants the group to continue, perhaps she never wants to address the pain of ending. Will our partners change? They may not. Is there any hope we can change anything?

The group is very involved with their need for a relationship which does not leave them powerless. The conductor feels drawn in, striving to understand his thoughts, feeling guilty at being unable to give the group the answer it seems to be searching for, unable to offer it hope. There is a longing for something better, but no hope of changing anything. How do we accept our parents? If we change, does that change them? Is death the only solution to ambivalence about parents, about the group?

At the next session the conductor forgets to look for messages, sits next to the bereaved person, and later has fantasies of comforting her. The conductor is caught up in acting out, in both action and thought, the conflicts of the previous week.

The conductor knows his emotions are aroused as he resonates with the group but fails adequately to understand what led to his acting out the countertransference. He stays silent this week, aware he is caught up in the group process.

> The interplay between the group and outside life is addressed through a member who has a new job and appears to have left early. The group decides it is the individual's choice to come or not, and the conductor should not contact him. The thought of change in one person leads to a review of what people have gained in the group, and their disappointments with how little has changed. So much has not been discussed, in particular members must protect others from their sadness. How attached have people been to the group? Is it in contacts outside the group that members have revealed more of themselves? Are people noticed in the group? Are we special to each other? Someone wonders if they will be remembered when dead.

This is a turning point, someone is angry with the defensiveness of the group, and new issues emerge.

> One person is jealous of others being special. Were we chosen for this group? Another wanted to be in this group as she fancied the conductor. One person suggests we are all special but only because we need to be here. This group solution is challenged: denying individuality, putting everyone down is not a solution to feeling guilty at wanting to be special, and envious of those who are. In the group there is a pull between being special to the conductor or the group. (A replay of the middle phase of the group.)

As this group addresses termination, there is a review of both the events in the group, and a replaying of the group process often with very intense emotions being expressed. There is anger with the conductor and a wish for another leader, Joan, who might not end it. There is a longing for closeness, bitter disappointment, and the question around will we be remembered, will anything last? The conductor is emotionally pulled about as much as the members, all using well-tried defences to reduce the distress and emotion of the ending.

There is a movement away from dependence on the conductor, a feeling people should make their own decisions, take responsibility for themselves. With this change more risks can be taken in the group: there is less fear of, as well as less time for, retaliation.

Review of the mature phase of group development

Theoretical discussion

At any phase in the group's development the group may revert to old practices which seem to belong to earlier stages of the group. The mature group begins, after a break, by running through several phases in rapid succession. Later there is a return to a preoccupation with being a special person in the group.

The group process illustrates a number of group therapeutic factors, which are discussed in Chapter 6. As it moves from attempting to solve the group patient Valerie's problems to associating freely with members resonating with each other, it is able to make use of its resources more fully than before. A similar stage will be reached in a more structured group or in a group whose purpose is other than for therapy. The group will develop and focus more effectively on its task, needing to spend less time and energy on extraneous matters which are often brought in, as we have seen, for defensive purposes.

This same session also raises an interesting question about the actual gender of the conductor. Most of the men are absent following an acknowledgement in the previous group that the women would like to have more contact with them. Valerie's problem is presented as an all-female issue to a predominantly female group. Yet for the experience to be therapeutic the intervention of the male conductor is necessary. Would the same processes have occurred with a female conductor?

The group is exploring deeper levels of communication. Foulkes (1964) described **four levels of communication** occurring in a group and here we have examples of three of these four levels. There is the level of **current reality**, where the conductor has been absent for a week. The **transference** level where links are made between a whole person and another in the group: for example, the conductor is treated as if he were the group member's father or mother. The level of **part object relations** is where splitting rather than repression is the primary defence as when Diana recognises a split-off part of herself which she fears to address.

Once again we see how the conductor is drawn into the group process and has to use his countertransference to try to understand what might be happening.

LEARNING POINTS

- **Recognising the mature group**

  A group which has established itself has a way of working together and recognising its identity as a group. Even when it appears to be chaotic or reverting to old defensive patterns it can usually be encouraged back into using its full resources.

  Moving towards its ending, the group replays past phases but this should not be mistaken for a real regression as it will return to its full capacity quite quickly.

- **Group-specific phenomena**

  The mature group members will be increasingly able to use specific group phenomena such as mirroring to foster growth and insight.

- **Using the countertransference**

  The group's intense emotional life makes great demands on the group conductor who may feel taken over by emotion. Whereas in earlier groups the conductor may have to intervene and facilitate communication, at this stage when group members may be providing many comments and interpretations, the conductor concentrates on his own internal responses. When the conductor is uncomfortable with his actions (that is, he suspects that the dynamic of the group is pulling him out of role) he can restrain himself from intervening and concentrate on trying to understand what his uncharacteristic behaviour may mean. Even the most experienced group conductor may seek supervision to elucidate his own experience in the group.

The Final Session

The period between the group's maturing and having to work through its ending was brief but the group was able to replay some of its earlier history, acknowledge its shortcomings and achievements and mourn its loss.

> Sitting in the lengthening silence the conductor wonders how to address the issues: breaking a silence can so easily be defensive, so easily shape the group for the conductor's peace of mind. As if in response to these thoughts, voices emerge talking of feeling upset, commenting on how the group has been, how it will be missed and wanting it to go on.

The conductor's work so far has been internal. He thinks about the silence and the meaning of his desire to break it which must reflect the difficulties that the group members are also having in facing the emotions generated by the ending of the group.

> A shadow suddenly passes across this rosy haze as Pauline angrily describes being betrayed by another: their hopes of friendship continuing after the group are dashed. She now wants nothing to do with anyone here, the group is totally destructive! The group is confronted with critical aspersions that members have made about others' professions.
>
> Various boundary incidents which have occurred through the life of the group are reported. The conductor suggests these are emerging now as the opportunities for resolving feelings outside the group are no longer available.

Under pressure the group is returning to its well-tried defensive style (basic assumption) of fight or flight. The group members focus on an aggressive interaction which makes people want to run away and thus enables them to avoid their inner conflicts. Only when Pauline describes herself as a scapegoat, and subgroups slowly emerge offering support to different people's feelings, does any reflection occur. Pauline has been pushed into playing a defensive role which has benefited the group and taken her out of it. The group joins together recognising their disappointment with the relationships here, and links are made to parents and the conductor.

> As the group ends Kingston expresses his sadness, and despite the jokes, draws others into acknowledging their own sadness. In the final moments it becomes clear it is not only the men who have been cautious at being involved in the group. With this there is a recognition of the need for regressive and narcissistic defences for the individual self to survive in the group situation.

5

WORKING IN THE GROUP

Part 1: Negotiating the boundaries

Introduction

Once a line has been drawn around the group defining its membership, the conductor will consider the implications of moving across the group boundary as people join and leave, the group has breaks and there are absences. We use the example of the group in Chapter 4 to look at the aspect of the conductor's task which Foulkes defined as **dynamic administration** leaving the discussion of her **therapeutic activity** for Chapter 6.

Joining the Group

Managing the boundary in the first group

Joining a new group arouses ambivalent feelings; members have invested hope and trust in the conductor and the therapeutic process but they bring their previous disappointments and memories of past responses to new situations. The degree of anxiety depends partly on the conductor's style, activity, and therapeutic approach. In daily life, for instance in a new reception class at a primary school, the teacher tries to create a situation that reduces anxiety.

In a group-analytic group the anxiety can be explored; the experience may be frustrating as the conductor fails to meet the dependency needs of the members, fails to show or tell them what to do. The members will push, cajole, bully and seduce the others as they try to make themselves less anxious. In these interactions (as we saw in Chapter 4 with Kingston and Valerie) much is revealed about the nature of the members' transferences to one another. Long-established behavioural patterns emerge. In other types of group, which do not use the anxiety for therapeutic ends in this way, enabling structures, such as warm-ups or ice-breakers, require members to express their anxieties and fantasies directly (for example, turn to your neighbour and say what your hopes and fears about the group are). Alternatively they proffer a structure in which members can quickly get to know each other (tell your partner one thing you'd like others in the group to know about you, or more light-heartedly, walk around the room greeting everyone in the manner of an animal which expresses something special about you).

While the new members are ambivalent the conductor holds the belief that membership of a group can be therapeutic. She sees how the individual and the group interrelate so that, with her help, a group of individuals becomes a creative and therapeutic enterprise. She has a special role, and is never an equal member of the group. In any group (ranging from an analytic therapy group to a brief social skills group) at the start, she becomes the object of transference, one aspect of which is to be an authority figure. Her transference role is reinforced because she is responsible for the group itself, and its relationship with the host organisation. How she chooses to work with her authority and the transference will depend on the aims of the group. She can direct the thinking of the members of the group, as in cognitive therapy, or use it to educate the group to take an interest in its own processes in an analytic group.

This will be the first time these people have met together, or if the conductor has taken over an ongoing group, the first time the group has this membership. There is an excitement, expectations and anxiety associated with something new. The conductor also needs to consider how her expectations may influence her behaviour and, through her, the group. In Chapter 4 the conductor monitored his countertransference, differentiating between feelings that emerged in response to the group meeting, and those that resulted from his anxieties, stemming from his previous experience of groups.

The first session of the group

The importance of establishing the boundaries for the group to become cohesive, creating a safe situation where trust can develop, has been discussed. There must be enough pressure so that people interact (not normally a problem in a first group), but not so much anxiety that members need to establish rigid defensive solutions to survive. The anxiety decreases as the group develops, a culture emerges, and defences arise to contain feelings. The first session offers a unique opportunity to observe the interaction of the members.

The start of the group in Chapter 4 shows how the conductor's weak planning heightened the group members' anxieties and led to an attempt at scapegoating. Had the conductor explained his mistakes he might have lowered the group temperature but would have lost some of the intensity of the individual members struggling to find a way to be together.

Either the conductor has failed to set up the room (pulls in another chair), or has added another member. 'This group is rather large.' The subject is raised immediately. The boundaries of the group are insecure, and become an issue as the group discuss confidentiality. Kingston is at risk of being scapegoated: the members are irritated with the conductor, and Kingston is indirectly addressing the issue.

Kingston might have been scapegoated because the uncertainties in the group make members afraid to confront the conductor. If this happens, at an early stage, unexpressed feelings will be lost to the group, basic trust compromised, and the member may be harmed.

The conductor acts to link Kingston's communication and Kingston himself to the group. A group interpretation would not be appropriate as there is not yet enough cohesion in the group. The communication moves on, others become involved, there is an increase in trust and revelations.

The conductor's intervention leads to a turning point; the group is established. With the formation of the group, awareness of others emerges.

Two members talk of knowing each other from elsewhere. The need for trust and the doubtful basis for relationships to develop in this group emerge.

As trust develops shameful incidents are addressed, anxiety increases as the group reaches another turning point, with increasing intimacy. The group is defining the nature of attachments, of boundaries. This produces cohesion in the group, but also a feeling of potential exposure and threat as members bring more of themselves across the group boundary. A **restrictive solution** develops. This gives temporary relief from tension in the group but leads away from further exploration of the currently difficult issue. In a non-analytic group a similar process will take place often facilitated by a graduated series of steps set out by the group conductors rather than relying on the interaction of group members and conductor seen earlier.

LEARNING POINTS

■ Establishing the group's boundaries is an important part of the conductor's therapeutic role.

■ The conductor needs to be aware of how the boundaries will affect the group from the very first session.

Working at the Boundary

The conductor has only begun her job when she brings the group into its first session. Now she has to enhance the holding and containing functions of the group boundary. Establishing appropriate boundaries involves members giving up some personal autonomy to the group and agreeing a structure and principles of conduct that enable the group to address its task.

Members want to change but, fearful of what the group may do to them, also want to stay as they are. Individually and collectively they may surprise the conductor by *misbehaving* and trying to bend the shape of the boundaries to suit old jigsaws. What is she to do? Tell them off?

Foulkes (1975) wrote about the **group-analytic situation** which is made up of the **conditions set** (which we have considered) and the **principles of conduct** required. 'By contrast to "conditions set", which are laid down by the therapist, "principles of conduct required" are based on the understanding of the group members, and are acquired through social learning in the group so that they will be respected and become a tradition of the group.' Foulkes was clear that there was no point in *telling* members to behave themselves like this, or remonstrating with them if they did not. The first prerequisite for this learning is that the conductor models or demonstrates their importance by maintaining them herself.

The group boundary is challenged from the outside by the organisation and outside activities of the members; and from the inside by the members' needs to reduce the tension of group membership. The conductor does all she can to guard and define the outside boundary of the group-analytic situation. Attempts to break the framework from within also call upon her function as the dynamic administrator of the group. The emphasis on *patrolling* or monitoring the boundary is based on the assumption that boundary breaking has a meaning which, if exposed and understood, can become part of the therapeutic experience. This understanding applies to analytic and non-analytic groups alike, once the nature of the boundary has been established.

This inner boundary addresses the principles of conduct required, which Foulkes has listed.

PRINCIPLES OF CONDUCT REQUIRED

- Regularity
- punctuality
- discretion
- abstinence
- no outside contact.

Clinical example

The importance of coming every week and turning up on time may seem obvious but, assuming the group consists of people who can organise themselves to attend regularly and on time, patterns of lateness and absence will reveal much about the members.

> A woman who has cared for others most of her life, joins a group. Social services agree to provide a child minder for her disabled child, but fail to organise it. This woman, who is very capable at arranging people and institutions to care for others, is unable to do this for herself. If she is to have treatment and help from others, she considers they should arrange everything, total responsibility must be taken for her as she does for others. Her behaviour defines a major focus for therapy.

If the members of the group are not able to organise themselves to attend regularly, or are attending to address their disorganisation, it is important that the group structure is adapted appropriately. In a reminiscence group for the elderly, part of the staff's task will be to offer an appropriate level of encouragement to ensure that the group members arrive at the group session. In this example attendance of itself is a therapeutic aim.

Discretion relates to **confidentiality** and respect for the other members. **Abstinence** means avoiding any tension-reducing *action* during a session – like smoking, eating, drinking or physical contact. Groups require *suspended action*; talking groups are where feelings are put into words rather than *acted out*. Abstinence is also necessary if someone is addicted to substances or a behaviour which they wish to understand. Everyone uses recurrent, established behaviours to avoid addressing feelings.

Record of group-analytic sessions

No. Place and time of meeting	Type of group		REMARKS

	Session no.
Year	Day
	Month
Therapist	
Attendance quotient	No. attended
	Total no.
Patients' names (see back of form for details)	

Symbols:
/ Present   L Late
– Absent by agreement   O Absent unexpectedly

There is always a balance to be established between acting to make sure that one is physically comfortable and can be fully present in the group session, and acting to withdraw from the immediacy of the group, defending against its challenges. Perhaps this dilemma is heightened when a member wants to make a life change such as taking a new job, or getting divorced. It is likely the group is influencing this decision which may require some exploration to discover whether this signifies a retreat from change or is necessary for the member to continue to develop in the group.

The principle of **no outside contact** refers to members meeting up outside the group and acting out inner states rather than trying to find words for them. An analytic group is not there to provide outside relationships but to widen people's options of *how* they relate to others. When members decide to go to the pub after a session (or join in some other social activity) they continue to behave as before. Transferences which have developed are short-circuited, acted out or resolved by well-tried psychological solutions, instead of being analysed and understood. The whole group is never involved in *after sessions* activity as the conductor is absent. When such events or meetings do take place they should be brought back to the group so that the feelings which engendered the action can be understood. Of course people meet by chance, where there is no attempt to manipulate the group, and these should also be reported in the group. If a free and open discussion occurs, vital information may emerge.

Some groups have different aims and consequently will set their boundaries differently. A group for pre- and post-natal parents has a double aim: to work through old conflicts and feelings which may be restimulated by the pregnancy and birth (like the analytic group); and to create a supportive social network for parents in their new families. The boundary round this group may include offering the group members some refreshment and encouraging them to meet outside the group.

Clinical example to clarify

Often the group members' outside contact expresses something they cannot address with the conductor, or another member. Verbalising their needs allows the group to look with them at what stops them communicating effectively in their everyday life.

> 'You were much more forthcoming, or authoritative. I saw you in a different light after our meeting in the...'
> 'Giving you a lift home, you said...'

'It seems mean to not offer you a lift when I go in that direction, but I feel we say a lot of things which should be said here, even though we do not discuss the group.'
'I have felt I have said much more since talking to you in the car, you bring things in for me.'

Pre- and post-group meetings do become part of the culture of the analytic group even though they are, by definition, outside the group boundary. Such meetings demonstrate the limits of the conductor's power; she cannot stop them without destroying the group. Their effective analysis is essential, and may involve the conductor learning much about herself (Hyde, 1991). As with other boundary issues the conductor has to continue to address them despite the group's irritation. 'We don't say anything important until you come in, it is only chatter.' The group may split off their concern for each other into the pre-group *chatter* leaving the group as a barren place of analysis.

Relationships that develop in the group

The survival of the group may be threatened in the extreme situation of an intimate relationship developing between two group members. The relationship is presumably an expression of affective need that is not being met, or probably even addressed in the group. This is one example of a common group defence where the affect is split off by the group, including the conductor, and projected into the selected members who act on the group's behalf, resolving it by acting out. The more actual sexual relationships develop in a group, the more difficult it becomes to discuss sexuality. The conductor should monitor any increase in the interest and interaction between two group members, helping the whole group to discuss their emotional and sexual feelings.

Patrolling the Boundary

The **conditions required** should not be presented as rules to be obeyed but as guidelines which are of interest to the group. It is through the conductor constantly considering **boundary issues**, addressing such 'non-problems' in the group as they arise, that members recognise the need for a clear structure. Anything a member does takes place in the context of the group as a whole, illustrating his own unique style of communication (jigsaw piece) which can be mapped out against the total network of communications (matrix) evolving in the group. The conductor does not tell people off for absences and latenesses, but tries to introduce and maintain a culture in which people are *interested* in the possible relevance and meaning of such events. By focusing on these boundaries, an *individual* action is reframed in a group context with the individual as the figure against the group background. It is equally important to have clearly defined (if different) boundaries in a non-analytic group so that this same process of giving meaning to the individual's experience within the group frame can take place. In the pre- and post-natal groups for parents regular attendance cannot be expected in the usual way as the baby's birth intervenes, but the group expectation that the parents will bring the newborn baby to the group holds the sense of the parents as group members in their absence; the new family is held in mind by the group.

Members also recognise their wish to have a group structure that meets their personal needs. This may involve breaking the structure. The individual and the group are in conflict about their need for the group to be therapeutic and the individual member's need to soothe his intrapsychic disturbance, that is, make himself feel better immediately. Through patrolling the boundary members become aware of their recurrent responses to situations, and begin to understand the reasons for their behaviour. Such work is making the unconscious conscious through addressing behavioural defences in the here and now, 'ego training in action' (Foulkes, 1964, p. 236).

Addressing boundaries is an ongoing task for the conductor and the group, but is particularly important at the beginning of the group.

A common way this conflict of needs emerges is through requesting an **individual meeting**, perhaps as a member leaves the room, on the phone or in letters. The request is a very real statement of need, and unless the conductor understands this and responds sensitively, a member may feel he has no option other than to drop out. There is a conflict of interests: the member wanting personal help, the conductor needing to develop and support the group as the vehicle in which therapy will occur. One way to respond is to invite the member to discuss the request in the group, for example, 'It is possible to meet, but perhaps we can discuss it in the group first.' Behind such a request is often a fear of saying something in the group. If the fear can be addressed in the group (the anxiety, perhaps about something shameful, or fearing a competitive response from other members), the individual meeting may no longer be needed. Allowing individual meetings with the conductor limits the potency of the group as it increases dependency on the conductor. Some groups are specifically set up to combine individual and group therapy, while in a therapeutic community setting group members will have contact during their daily lives in many different settings.

There are times in an analytic group when it is propitious for the conductor to break the 'conditions required', for example to see an individual. There may be personal therapeutic work needing to be addressed, or issues which will not be adequately addressed in the group. The conductor must decide if the individual session will support the integration of the group. If not, is the benefit for the individual greater than the harmful effect on the group?

Another way in which boundary issues are used defensively by group members is through denial. A group member who was upset the previous week is absent and the group members appear not to notice and to be absorbed in discussing another group member's serious problem at work. The conductor may easily be swayed into believing that the group is working hard and that it would be trivialising the work to mention the absence. Here, what may be being avoided is the group members' fear that if a group member is upset he may flee from the group so they all give the impression that they are members of a positive non-threatening and hard-working group. It is the conductor's task to remind the group of the apparently forgotten member and to help them to explore whatever is being denied.

Critical issues raised at the end of a session

The group-analytic structure has tight time boundaries: yet often critical and sometimes desperate matters are raised a few minutes before the group ends. Members know the time constraints and this behaviour must be understood as a communication. As the conductor focuses on the *process rather than the content* fundamental issues nearly always emerge and considerable insight is gained. But in the immediate crisis that emerges at the end of the group, the conductor must work with the group members to ensure that they feel understood and taken seriously, while keeping the time boundary. A situation which has clear boundaries will support the members' internal boundaries and their ability to feel contained.

Reasons for raising issues at the end of sessions may include: a member feeling his situation is hopeless; fearing other members will disapprove of him; feeling there has been no time for him to speak; frustration or anger with the conductor, the group, or his fellow members. Such behaviour should be analysed, as often it recurs.

Clinical example

Demonstrating a transference to the conductor.

> Three times, just before the end of the session, a man begins to movingly talk about his attempts to talk to his father, but his father always brings someone else along who gets in the way. As this was understood in the group and the connection was made between the group conductor ending the group and the father, the member was able to see his part in it and made a different contact with his father.

Implicit in all that has been said so far is that the conductor's task is to maintain a delicate tension or balance between the expressed needs of the individual member who may be saying 'I want to see you on my own', 'I will turn up late for the session', 'I will go to the pub after the group with John if I like him', and the needs of the group to pull together and to conform to certain norms if they are to be able to function at all. The conductor aims to create a group which will increasingly function effectively without her constant direct intervention. In a group-analytic therapy group or a working group (see Chapter 8) a matrix develops which allows the group to continue to function so that, for instance, in a working co-operative they find that when a seemingly indispensable individual leaves somehow another member steps in to fill his space. When the person who is always late leaves the group someone else usually takes over as the latecomer. Similar processes take place in a structured group in spite of the greater apparent dependence on the conductor.

Members or a conductor joining the group

It is difficult taking over a group from another conductor or joining a group as a new co-conductor. There is considerable tension as the conductor tries to establish her role and authority in a group (assuming it functions well) which, not having chosen her, will take responsibility for itself: the structure, boundaries and culture will be clear. As she negotiates her relationship with the group she will be helping them to address their loss (see section on ending). Unclear as to whether they need the intruder, the group may fear to express its anger towards her openly when their structure has so recently been threatened.

The new conductor offers the group an opportunity to address the inevitable limitations of the previous leader but it is important the new conductor does not devalue the old conductor. Whatever was not resolved may emerge with considerable emotion or as acting out. The hopes and fears aroused by her presence may lead the new conductor to make transference interpretations about her relationship to the whole group early on. This can be useful for an already established group.

The conductor will think about whether it is an appropriate time to introduce a new member into the group and will give the group the opportunity to air their feelings and fantasies. She appears to control entry to the group, but new people can only join if the boundary is permeable enough. Assessing the mood of the group to accept new members, and preparing the group for their arrival, is essential. There is a balance between the conductor who is responsible and takes the decision to actively introduce a new member and the power of the group matrix which will play an important part in determining how the entry will be.

The concept of the group providing a *good-enough* container for personal development can help to explain the strong emotions provoked by the conductor's demand that members integrate a potentially disturbing outsider. The fears of a new infant pushing one out of one's special position, or the joy of not being the new baby any longer may emerge. Under attack from the group, the conductor remembers that however much the present members protest, a new member may have benefits for them. The arrival allows present members to retrace their own experiences of arriving both in the group and in their own lives. A new member will bring his own new dimensions and themes into the group matrix. There is also excitement and expectation attached to what the new person may bring to each individual member and the group. Unconsciously, the conductor or the group may hope that the new member will be the solution to the group's difficulties (Bacha, 1997).

LEARNING POINTS

- The group conductor provides the boundaries or the **conditions set**. She works with the group members towards their understanding the importance and significance of both maintaining the boundaries and understanding the meaning when a boundary is broken. The conductor helps the group to think about the **principles required**.

- Group members begin to be interested when a boundary is broken and take on some of the responsibility for exploring the meaning of the action, although this may need to be supplemented by the conductor at times.
- A member often breaks a group boundary as a way of expressing something which he cannot yet put into words.
- A new conductor negotiates her relationship with an established group, exploring with them what it means to have lost the old conductor and to have her enter its boundaries.
- The conductor decides when it is appropriate for new members to join a group and helps the group members to understand what it means for them.
- The disturbance of having a new conductor or a new member in the group can lead to productive work for the existing members.

Separating from the Group

Holidays and absences

The conductor gives the group appropriate notice of her planned absence, even if the group meets without her. She expects members to make the group a priority and she shows them similar respect. These codes of behaviour and responsibility are applicable to all groups. She should ideally plan her absences and the group's breaks a year in advance. This forward planning invites exploration of the implications of individual members giving up some of their autonomy to the group, while in a time-limited group clear dates firm up the boundary. A minimum notice of absence is two weeks.

Giving notice of a break does not prevent a response, often of loss, disappointment or anger with the conductor for letting them down. These responses are not always expressed directly but provide an opportunity to explore the reaction to her absence: feelings about members when they are absent by arrangement or with no warning should be considered. Breaks are valuable to members; becoming aware that the group is not a permanent institution leads to reflection on their involvement and dependence on the group which are discussed on their return. It is invaluable for an established group to meet without the conductor, if this is organisationally possible, supporting the group to take responsibility for itself and challenging its dependency on the conductor: members behave differently when she is absent.

Leaving a group

In an ongoing group, if a member has moved through the stage of joining, to valuing the group where he can honestly explore feelings and relationships, to finding such relationships in his outside life, he is ready to leave. The group will have become less important: until the date for leaving is fixed!

Other members do not reach this ideal, but, aware that their life has changed, want to move on. Foulkes (1964, p. 236) was clear that therapy should not continue for too long: 'If some success has been sustained in helping the patient translate his symptoms into his problems or in helping him to see what has been preventing him from solving his own problems, then a great deal has been achieved.'

Both scenarios are different from the individual who suddenly departs. Soon after joining the group, the member feels threatened, the tension becomes unbearable and the only solution seems to be to leave. Often he has been unable to express something, or felt he has said too much and is no longer acceptable to the group. The flight may be from sexual feelings, a transference situation or a flight into health. Sometimes an individual session enables the member to rejoin the group.

In an ongoing group, a member is encouraged to discuss the idea of leaving before fixing a date. This can be difficult as envy and rivalry emerge or fears of being left behind in the group, without him, confusing the group members' rational assessment of this person's progress. The aim is to understand if his leaving is a defensive solution to what is happening in the group, or a creative action for him; but it brings up a concentrated review of his relationships in the group. When a date is set it should allow him to take advantage of this opportunity. A minimum length of time would be four weeks. With established as well as recent members leaving is often rationalised, practical reasons being produced to avoid addressing their loss, the disappointments and the fears. No member exists in isolation and loss of a member means the loss of them in all their different group roles. The whole group has to mourn the loss.

While some of these decisions are avoided by a closed group with a fixed termination date (like the group in Chapter 4) the mourning still takes place at the end of the group. People often leave before the end raising both practical problems about what to do with a shrinking group and the necessity of understanding their premature departures.

Conductors and co-conductors, like members, move away, are ill, can no longer continue. Much emerges as the meaning of the loss for the members and the conductor is explored. The conductor may at such times feel frail, just like the group members, when asked to negotiate such difficult issues within the group.

Endings in Groups

Endings and beginnings

A fundamental aspect of human development involves leaving behind one period of life and moving on to another. Negotiating these turning points enables a person to move effectively through the developmental phases of life brought about by physiological and psychosocial changes. The failure to negotiate endings effectively is one of the key causes of intrapsychic and interpersonal difficulties.

Leaving a group offers a unique opportunity to address these issues again. Whether it be *forced* by the group's sudden ending, or the conductor's departure; the whole group ending by previous agreement; one person leaving by agreement; or being left behind when another member leaves – there is a dramatic change in the group structure and often members become quite disturbed. The group process is accelerated with a sense of time running out. Issues that members have feared to raise are addressed while the group is still alive. The conductor must work with the group to use these opportunities in the interests of the individuals and the group.

Separation from the group will be the most recent of a number of separations for the members. Present experience resonates with the past in a disturbing manner, depending on the individual's previous attempts to address separation and loss. A group or individual may respond to this intensification of feeling by using old defensive solutions. Often it seems nothing has been achieved as patterns of behaviour and symptoms re-emerge that members have left behind long ago. It helps for the conductor to be aware that the considerable regression is usually temporary and indicates that work on the ending is under way (Maar, 1989; Wardi, 1989).

There is an underlying assumption that many group members have had difficulties with early separations which have reverberated throughout their lives. Bowlby (1979) thought that many of the most intense emotions arise during the formation, maintenance, disruption and renewal of attachment relationships. Anxiety over separation is normal, but if the separation is forced upon the individual, pathological anxiety may also occur. He described the anxiously attached as responding to loss by anger, or self-reproach and depression; the compulsively self-reliant respond to loss with anxiety and guilt. Kauff (1977) considered that the nature and outcome of the early separation from the mother determines the adult's subsequent experience with termination, linking termination in the group to the separation-individuation phase of development in the infant. The child needs a dependable frame of reference to cope with the joy of growing autonomy and the loss of infantile grandiosity. The group, having an existence separate from that of its members, provides an opportunity for exploring the rapprochement phase of development when the child needs to move away and return to that frame, without being either rebuffed or engulfed.

When the relationship with the mother is unsatisfactory during this period she cannot contain the infant's struggle and object representations are split. As traces of this period of early development arise in the current group, similar defensive solutions emerge. Splitting into opposites is prevalent during the termination phase of therapy. There is idealisation (the omnipotence of the small child knowing adults are there just for her) and devaluation. Winnicott (1982) emphasised the importance of the therapist surviving the maximum destructiveness of the patient if the therapist is to be more than the projection of part of the patient.

Working through in the group

Group therapy has unique potential for making the stressful period of an ending a productive one.

Aggression towards the *destructive* therapist and feelings from previous losses surface in the closed group in Chapter 4:

> Members become aware of the rapid approach of the end of the group. They are shocked by the sadism of one member who pierces slugs on knitting needles to protect the tender young shoots in her garden... Diana becomes aware of what she has not done. She speaks of... how the conductor's absence aroused feelings... about her father.

The group holds two opposing feelings. The conductor, the group and the individual members are available as objects for projection; together they provide the necessary containment and integrate the projections.

'It's only now five years after my father died I realise how much I've lost!' The contrasting view is expressed by Joan who considers: 'Perhaps she can now be free and get on with her own life.'

An ongoing group tangibly and visibly survives rejection by a departing member. It remains, knowing the individual, holding the internal objects which that member has projected into it. It has the potential to act as a *transitional object* the first *not me* possession which marks the infant's transition from the symbiotic state to the differentiated state where reality testing and objectivity reign (Winnicott, 1982). The group provides that alternative area between fantasy and reality, in which the departing member may again address issues of separation.

The ambivalence of being in the group emerges. An unconscious wish to recover a previous narcissistic equilibrium may have interfered with a conscious desire for change. Idealisation acts as a defence against individuation and grief. When the end is in sight, reality challenges the fantasy that the longed-for narcissistic equilibrium has been recovered. The fantasy now has to be relinquished.

Every group which is working through issues of loss and ending will go through similar phases of mourning to those experienced at a death:

- initial denial
- anger, which may be expressed or acted out
- depression
- acceptance.

If this is to enable the group member to move on, then the conductor and the group need actively to address the loss that is faced. Initial denial may involve plans to follow the therapist, establish a personal relationship with her. This may occur surreptitiously by identification, taking up therapy as a career, dressing or talking in a similar manner. In this example the conductor's existence is also denied.

The group wants to continue in the following year, and to appoint one of its members as the therapist. There is a wish to avoid the reality of the ending, maintain an omnipotent fantasy and in particular provide the desired narcissistic equilibrium for one of its members.

Anger must be owned. As the group notes what has not been achieved it feels let down by the conductor in particular; the group has been a disappointment. Much would happen if only there were a little more time. Splitting must be addressed and both the positive aspects of therapy and the disappointments owned. Reviewing their history in the group, and being challenged to integrate emotions, leads to depression as members own to their part in destroying a now much longed-for experience. There is a new sense of loss and moving on into an altered life.

> The thought of change in one person leads to a review of what people have gained in the group, and their disappointments with how little has changed. So much has not been discussed, in particular members must protect others from their sadness. How attached have people been to the group?... Are people noticed in the group? Are we special to each other? Someone wonders if they will be remembered when dead.

In all this the conductor herself will have to contend with the resonances with her own experience of separation and loss and how she has resolved them. She may be tempted to avoid focusing on the process especially when the group become critical of her, appear to have made no changes or sink into despair. It can become difficult to maintain the necessary detachment to effectively observe the group process.

> The conductor wishes to comfort the bereaved person and at another point feels guilty at being unable to give the group the answer for which it is searching... The conductor knows his emotions are aroused as he resonates with the group the previous week. He stays silent in the group as he becomes aware he is caught up in the group process. Failure to understand adequately what happened the previous week in the group leads to his acting out in the countertransference. The acting out... gives clues to the underlying conflict.

Understanding the therapeutic potential of the ending, knowing what to expect and working on her personal associations to endings can help her to use her countertransference more effectively. All group conductors need this awareness, although, of course, like the beginning of a group, the ending must be addressed according to the group's aim.

LEARNING POINTS

- The conductor is responsible for the group's timetable and tries to plan it showing respect for the group members.
- The conductor encourages the group members to acknowledge and recognise their feelings about breaks and absences so that this becomes an important part of the group's work.

■ The conductor needs to maintain her own awareness of what separation and ending may mean for her personally to help her to work with the group members' experiences.

■ Endings and breaks in the group involve both group members and the conductor in loss and mourning.

■ The conductor has the difficult task of staying in touch with the *value* of going through this painful process in the group as a way of working through personal unresolved losses and learning to mourn.

Summary

As people, their energy, presence and emotions move across the boundary of the group the members resonate in their personal ways to the issues which arise. Turbulence at the boundary challenges the group system, forcing it and its members to explore new experiences, or use old defensive strategies. Much of the therapeutic potential of group therapy arises from these boundary incidents which are far from being a mere disturbance in the group's equilibrium. Equally important is a clear, firm and secure boundary to the group that allows trust and exploration, providing a frame which allows observation of the process and space for reflection. The dilemma the conductor and the group face is between allowing turbulence which is exciting and potentially allows growth, or developing a secure situation which is potentially limiting. The balance must be right for a particular group or individual at a particular time: it is always changing. The conductor, through patrolling the boundary, influences the permeability of the boundary and through this the therapeutic activity of the group.

6

WORKING IN THE GROUP

Part 2: Interventions and interpretations; therapeutic activity

Introduction

The group conductor has a crucial input to the **therapeutic activity** of the group, as well as to its dynamic administration. She thinks about what is happening in the group, between group members and within individuals; her initial interventions facilitate the group process rather than addressing an individual. The conductor's activity is influenced by her stance, her style, her orientation, her own past and present social location, her understanding of the group process, her expectations expressed both in the stated aims of the group and by her conscious and unconscious contributions.

As she enters the group, the conductor orientates herself, beginning to observe both the group and her own responses, preoccupied with the questions of what to do and when to act. *Why* should a conductor act? *How* should she intervene? *When* is the right time? The conductor needs to understand what is happening in the group. What unconscious processes are involved now, perhaps expressed by a particular group member? What she observes will enable her to plan her interventions.

She will think about whether her interventions promote the therapeutic potential of the group experience. Yalom's (1995) classic research on this subject led him to propose a list of factors which we examine and supplement with a group-analytic account of certain group phenomena and therapeutic factors.

Using the concepts and theories that underlie the group conductor's decisions she will consider how and when to offer interpretations and whether they are aimed at facilitating the group process (for the benefit of individual members), or when there is a need for individual interpretation. Group focal conflict theory and a systems model of group therapy offer developments in thinking about the whole group process and each individual's contribution to it which can clarify the conductor's difficult decisions about when and how to intervene in the group process. The chapter will draw on examples from the group described in Chapter 4 as well as considering how these ideas can be applied to other types of group.

The Conductor Orientates Herself in the Group

The conductor defines the boundary as she enters the group room.

> In an analytic group she glances around the room making brief eye contact with some people as she sits down, saying no more than hello.

This is the start of the group session. In a structured group the conductor may start by asking for feedback from the group members' homework or may wonder how they feel to be back in the group, but she will have a similar awareness.

> How does the atmosphere change as she walks in and sits down? Is there a sudden hush? Do people stop talking slowly or in a relaxed manner? Is there tension in the air? Who is silent? Who looks withdrawn? Is the room warm, light?

She works to place herself in the context of this particular group.

> Thinking about the organisational details, any planned absences, any information that should be passed on, she continues to orientate herself towards the group. Any messages given will be short and factual.

She attempts to place herself in the historical context as well as the current context of the group and of society as it impinges on the members.

> How does this group relate to the previous few groups? She notices and thinks about the individuals, what does she know about their past, about their current lives? How have they been getting on in the group? She attempts in her mind to address each of them as an individual.

The conductor brings her past and present network of relationships, including those within the institution where the group is held; through her, the context of the group will be reflected in its process. She is subject, like the other members, to the feelings and pressures that emerge in the group, within the dynamic matrix.

> She is expectant, excited, a bit anxious. She becomes aware of the feelings she is bringing into the group, wondering how they will affect her behaviour today. Like the conductor of the group in Chapter 4, ideas and emotions come into her mind. She examines her feelings for what they may tell her about the nature of the resistance, defences and conflicts in the group, particularly if the conflict is located with her.

The conductor will be influenced by her training, supervision and her own experience of being in groups. Current life events will make their mark on her specific personal history, her belief systems and her character traits. She brings all this into the group needing to observe and understand how it is influencing her and the group. She must be aware of her countertransference and understand why she will, at times, decide to analyse it openly in the group.

In Chapter 4, at the beginning of the group's final session, the conductor decided not to analyse his countertransference aloud in the group.

> Sitting in the lengthening silence the conductor wonders how to address the issues: breaking a silence can so easily be defensive, so easily shape the group for the conductor's peace of mind. As if in response to these thoughts, voices emerge talking of feeling upset, commenting on how the group has been, how it will be missed and wanting it to go on.

As group members begin to speak the conductor orientates herself to the therapeutic task, holding on to her perspective of what is therapeutic, based on theory and experience.

> She listens carefully to the members. The opening statements often define the themes of the session.

In an analytic group, the conductor wants the members to communicate with each other, resonating to what each says. Foulkes described this as **free floating discussion**. It is this process of building on what is said with something associated but different that deepens communication and understanding. Whether the group be analytic or structured, the conductor hopes one person's resonance to another offers a different perspective to all; interpretation happening through the process of communication, without her having to intervene.

> She watches for evidence that the flow of communication is being blocked. She may try and help the process by inviting people to give voice to their resonance. 'What does that bring to mind for others here?'

She is interested in who speaks when, noting the issues that a member is driven to respond to, aware this tells her much about the individual's psychological processes. As the free group association continues she notices that some people are more involved than others with the current theme. She is as interested in those who remain silent.

Seeing some members looking withdrawn and uninvolved, she is wondering what they are thinking. What is *not* being said in the group? Will this emerge? Will the conductor have to draw it out?

Discussion

Watching the conductor orientate herself in the group makes Foulkes' choice of the term group 'conductor' understandable. He likened the role to the orchestral conductor, who brings in the different voices that make up the harmony. The score is in the matrix of the group, and leadership roles become progressively shared between different members of the group. Each member may have the melody.

The conductor will intervene when her help is clearly needed. She may be more active in the early stages of the group, or at the beginning of each session. She encourages members' active participation, using and supporting their contributions. Throughout the group in Chapter 4 the conductor becomes less overtly active as he enables the group to work for itself.

In an analytic group it is up to the individual members to be understanding, respond to each other's distress, remember what has happened to each other, satisfy their needs. In a structured group the conductor may provide more direction. In any group where there is a lack of empathy or care the conductor will be wondering why. She will try to help the members become more involved with each other by understanding the **resistance** (see later) in the group. She encourages the group to take responsibility for itself. It is easy to be drawn into individual therapy, but such a response attacks both the principles and the effectiveness of group therapy.

In Chapter 4 the conductor explains to the group that they have become stuck treating Valerie as the group patient, trying to empathise and resolve Valerie's problems with her daughter and explains:

We can't know what the daughter feels or how she is. What we can know are Valerie's feelings as they are at this time in this group.

This intervention focused the group enabling them to move on, resonating to Valerie's feelings about her relationship with her mother with their own difficulties both with mothers and as parents.

The conductor may be active in the background, attempting to integrate the group processes in her own mind. In a structured group this may be particularly important since underlying processes are not part of the explicit group agenda and yet they need to be considered by the conductor.

> With the conductor having addressed and contained the projective identifications in himself, the group is also able to contain the anxiety around the move.

Here the conductor has to work hard and silently finding no reason for discussion or interpretation in the group. His decision proves right since the group neither fragments nor denies that the move has had an impact.

The conductor's orientation is to helping the group understand how the discussion of past events or matters outside of the group relate to the present dynamic processes within the group. She does not develop herself as a transference figure since, unlike in individual psychotherapy, the main working through of past relationships does not take place between the individual and the therapist.

THE CONDUCTOR'S ROLE

- Acts to maintain the structure, protecting it from collapse.
- Facilitates the development of the group, increasing understanding in the group, and the level at which the group is functioning. In a structured group this includes setting the structures.
- Increases communication, supporting the interaction of members.
- Makes use of events that occur in the group for the benefit of the group and the individuals in it.
- Monitors her countertransference.
- Interprets to the group and to individuals.
- Makes no immediate response, understanding and containing the group's anxiety or disturbance.
- Acts in a manner to maintain an appropriate level of anxiety, protect individuals, avoid doing harm and increase trust in the group.
- Self-discloses when appropriate.
- Models.
- Considers what errors she has made and how she should respond to them.

The Conductor Intervenes to Enhance the Therapeutic Factors in the Group

The conductor needs to recognise those group phenomena and factors which enable a group to become a therapeutic space. They occur in all groups. The conductor's choice of which processes she emphasises and reinforces to increase the therapeutic potential of the group varies according to its aims and theoretical orientation. Skill-based groups will focus on **imparting information**; a group for survivors of sexual abuse will address the ways in which members feel isolated by their trauma (see **universality** later); psychodrama emphasises the value of **catharsis**.

Yalom (1995) summarised the research into what constitute therapeutic factors in a group. Yalom argues that these factors become an 'organising principle' in the therapist's approach.

The conductor tries to increase the expression of the relevant factors which harness the integrative potential of the group for its therapeutic purpose. Readers may find it useful to think about familiar groups and consider which of these factors are particularly important.

A group for unemployed young people may **instill hope** and may encourage them to see that they have something worthwhile to offer and are valued by others (**altruism**). In the early days, the group in Chapter 4 felt hopeless; it clung to Valerie's hopes about moving to the country until it could see potential in the group. It discovered the value of sharing experiences. Indirectly the conductor imparted information about this and about the importance of paying attention to the group boundaries.

YALOM'S THERAPEUTIC FACTORS

- Instillation of hope
- universality
- imparting information
- altruism
- the corrective recapitulation of the primary family group
- development of socialising techniques
- imitative behaviour
- interpersonal learning
- group cohesiveness
- catharsis
- existential factors.

In a group for people who have difficulty in making social connections, the format of the group may be *teaching social skills* with discussions of a video or a role play. The participants will learn both from the formally presented material (imparting information) and from the experience of being in a group where the interactions between people can be facilitated and examined (**development of socialising techniques**). The group conductor may be aware that the source of many group members' problems lies in their early experience in the family; while not making transference interpretations or developing a group discourse with an easy flow between past and present (as in an analytic therapy group) she may note these connections, helping a participant, where appropriate, to connect his fear of speaking to anyone in authority with his interactions with his father. Thus the conductor of a structured group may make use of its capacity for **the corrective recapitulation of the primary family group**. In the group in Chapter 4 there are several instances where group members connect what is happening in the present with experiences within their families.

A group brings people face to face with others, recognising similarities, reducing isolation and the associated tension. Yalom termed this most basic aspect of being in a group universality. It is important in homogeneous groups where people come together around the very difficulty which isolates them, for example, survivors of sexual abuse or those who have had neurosurgery. In the early part of the Chapter 4 group's life the conductor was working hard to encourage Kingston, who had isolated himself, to fit into the group and thus increase its **cohesion**; this may be defined as the attraction of the group for the members and the members for the group. A cohesive group is more likely to have good attendance and intense relationships. The conductor waited to tell his group about the impending move until they had established more cohesion. Pines (1985) suggests that a cohesive group can become one with impermeable boundaries which may resist change while an analytic group will develop **coherence** through the members' self-organisation rather than through a structure imposed by the conductor. While this allows for an optimal level of relatedness (which is what the analytic group aims for), in a structured group, such as the group for agoraphobics in Chapter 1, the conductors work to build a cohesive group which is able to weather the challenges set by the group's tasks.

Group members may model themselves on each other or on the conductor; this **imitative behaviour** expresses their sense of belonging. In both analytic and structured groups one group member may try a mode of behaviour or way of speaking copied from another. Once one man has cried in a group, others may break the social taboo too. Imitative behaviour may also be defensive, avoiding personal exploration and masking unacceptable or negative feelings.

Group members need to feel free to express strong emotions. In a group, resonance with another member may lead to a sudden welling up of affect, and awareness of unrecognised or unconscious feelings. Catharsis or expressing pent-up emotion often makes people feel better. But some members may use the group as a place to discharge their emotions without reflection. This is similar to acting out the affect and change is unlikely.

> In the last session of the group in Chapter 4 Pauline's expression of rage, feeling betrayed by a 'friend' in the group leads to her attacking and devaluing the group for herself. There is a loss of trust.

It is not the discharge of emotion which produces change, but what happens in response to the expression of intense feeling. In groups using techniques which positively encourage catharsis such as psychodrama, Gestalt groups and bio-energetics, the conductor needs to ask whether the strong expression of emotion also leads to increasing trust within the group. Do others resonate with it? Does it move the group to a new level of understanding or a turning point?

As group members lose their feelings of isolation the group can provide a frame which addresses **interpersonal** learning. In a group whose primary task is to help its agoraphobic members to overcome their phobia, interpersonal learning is present and contributes to its success, but will not be highlighted. However, the conductors may consciously use the group setting to facilitate interaction knowing it is one aspect of the agoraphobic's difficulties. In an analytic group interpersonal learning is central.

> Georgina (in the group in Chapter 2) felt upset and envious when another woman was being cared for by one of the men. She began to see the benefits of interacting with others and what she lost by not doing so.

Group analysis describes the need for a balance between **integrative** and **analytic** forces in a group. Integrative work precedes effective analytic work so that anxiety and defensiveness do not overwhelm the group. The primary school teacher develops a structure within which her class can work, otherwise all the creative and learning activities will be diminished.

At *turning points* in the group when there is a major shift in the style or level of functioning in the group there may be a highly charged expression of emotion. An awareness of sharing and struggling together (universality), a sense of hope, a desire to help each other, enables group members to face the inevitable narcissistic wounds or lack of safety that the individual feels as he uncovers his inner world. This is also why it is important to compose a group carefully so that there are not too many isolates in terms of social and external factors. It is important to address differences (such as race or disability) explicitly so that they become part of the group's discourse, encouraging the development of universality.

Group-analytic therapeutic factors and group phenomena

The factors summarised by Yalom (1995) as being therapeutic in groups, can be incorporated into the group-analytic perspective. Foulkes identified **communication** as being the crucial therapeutic aspect of group life and noted several group phenomena which could enhance communication, of which we will consider two: **resonance** and **mirroring**.

'Working towards an ever more articulate form of communication is identical to the therapeutic process itself' wrote Foulkes (1948, p. 169). He believed that facilitating the process rather than the content of communication within the group defined why, when and how the conductor should intervene. The symptom, which leads a person to a therapy group, is an autistic communication crying out to be heard, but unable to be understood either by the person themselves, or those with whom they relate. The symptom 'mumbles to itself secretly, hoping to be overheard; its equivalent meaning conveyed in words is social' (Foulkes and Anthony, 1957, p. 259). The therapeutic task is to translate the symptom into an understandable communication, so that the subject is no longer isolated and withdrawn and there is increasingly free and open communication within the group.

In Chapter 4 we saw how as one member of a group speaks it strikes a chord in others, their response adding a personal timbre to the sound of the group.

As Valerie expands on the awful relationship between her mother and herself, others resonate and share their feelings and difficulties with... themselves as parents... Others share their experience of caring for aging parents. The group develops a wish just to leave their families behind and go off on a powerful motorbike. Perhaps the bike owned by the one man in this session. But none of the women has a motorbike.

Foulkes, noting this phenomenon, termed it 'resonance'. Each individual reacts in his or her own specific, idiosyncratic manner to issues that arise, enriching and deepening the emotional experience of the group. Within a group each member may recognise aspects of herself mirrored in another.

> The increasing irritation between a man and a woman is commented on by others. Pushed by the man, she owns to being repulsed by him. It is the way he shows his neediness. She is suddenly shocked by the statement she has just made. The group contrasts the statement with the self-control she normally shows. The man is not put down by her attack, and happily owns to this aspect of himself. As she talks she realises she despises the neediness in herself, and begins to recognise the side of herself which has been split off and projected into this man.

Initially recognising feared or rejected parts of oneself in another begins the process of owning those aspects of oneself.

In the group a member resonates to another's contribution, becoming aware of a different aspect of herself. There is identification with others. A natural aversion or hostility to another member may emerge; a part of themselves is mirrored in the other. The members learn that in observing and tolerating others' behaviour, they are working on themselves, learning to accept a split-off aspect of the self which is projected into the other. The group becomes a hall of mirrors reflecting, amplifying, and distorting the members' images of themselves.

Groups share the aim of translating the symptom into another mode of expression which is less harmful for the group member; whether this be enacting a crucial emotional scene in psychodrama or a de-conditioning exercise in a behaviour therapy group. The conductor will be aware of identification and mirroring in the group.

Thinking About and Intervening in Group Processes

As the conductor facilitates the aspects of group life which enhance its therapeutic potential at times the flow of communication appears to be blocked. The conductor needs to understand the meaning of the resistance and how it can best be addressed in this group. Is this group behaving as it has done before, or exploring issues it has addressed as in the past? How useful has that been? We have found in our work with non-analytic groups that these questions need to be addressed lest ignoring the underlying resistance blocks the ability of the group to carry on with its task.

Processes which may limit the group include, classifying a sub-group of people and attacking them, scapegoating, finding an identified patient to cure, questioning another member as if drawing out that member will express everything that is happening for the whole group (see example, Chapter 4, one person monopolising the group while others listen silently).

Role suction or personification in the group

At the beginning of the group in Chapter 4 Kingston seems to be the only group member who feels anxious. Is he being *sucked* into playing a role on behalf of the whole group? The conductor, recognising that the group may be resisting becoming aware of their anxieties and seeing the blockage in communication, the potential for scapegoating, coupled with the lack of a developed group culture (or matrix), decides to make a firm intervention. He speaks through one member to the whole group:

> 'Kingston hopes the group will respect him if he explores aspects of himself he does not respect.'

The conductor's indirect reference to Kingston taking on the group's burden releases the group members to share their experience of the new group.

Kingston returns to the foreground when the group hears that their venue is to be changed, arousing similar anxieties and uncertainties. The conductor wonders if Kingston is compelled to repeat an unresolved past situation and how this relates to the group's difficulties in proceeding. Thinking that perhaps the two come together in an ambivalence about intimacy he comments that 'Kingston fears being penetrated by the group'. The interpretation succeeds in removing Kingston from his central position, but confuses the group. The conductor wonders whether he, too, was caught up in the group projection and was expressing his own fears of being penetrated by the group's anxieties. The group is strong enough to weather the experience by temporarily reducing tension through focusing on outside events. This is partly achieved through a division into subgroups with one subgroup offering a 'solution' of self-sufficiency.

Subgroups

Exploring issues in subgroups allows members to focus on one emotion while other, often opposite, emotions are experienced by a different subgroup. Be it a practical issue such as should one work, or a more intensely emotional issue such as feeling sad following your mother's death, there is a *differentiation* of emotions. In Chapter 4, the subgroups are initially polarised around male/female stereotypes where men distance themselves and women want to be close. As the group develops the members begin to see how the other subgroup mirrors the very aspects of themselves they find it hard to accept. *Integration* of this sort takes place as differences are recognised and are allowed to co-exist. The conductor watches the subgrouping to see whether it promotes the flow of communication or seems to be stuck. Will this be a creative and integrative process or one that limits further exploration of the current issue? When integration does not appear to be taking place, she may need to intervene.

Silent people in the group

The conductor is as interested in silent, withdrawn and uninvolved members as those who talk. What is *not* being said in the group? Will this emerge? Will she have to draw it out? She watches the silent people for clues that they are ready to communicate. If she senses that people want to talk but the group is ignoring them she wonders whether there are tensions between members, or the group cannot give voice to what the silent members could express. Perhaps the silence is a resistance because the material is too deep or disturbing. The conductor may intervene to establish a balance in the group enabling integration to occur. As the temporarily silent people voice what has been repressed, the group can explore at deeper levels.

> A man joins a group. Despite his silence he is clearly part of the group. Confrontation occurs when he suggests he would like to have a relationship with a woman. 'You are gay!' the group exclaims. In a **group role perspective** he confirms for the other group members that sexual orientation is fixed absolutely, for life; as soon as he breaks his silence and wants to explore his sexual orientation, the group members have to consider questioning their sexual orientation.

Given support, with the advantage of their observer position, the silent member often makes an invaluable contribution.

If a silent member talks when the conductor is away, it suggests that the anxiety and defences are *located* in his relationship with the conductor. The group may help the member understand this or the conductor may need to actively intervene.

A wholly silent group may be productively reflective, or responding appropriately to what is occurring; perhaps the conductor has made a plunging or inappropriate interpretation. The conductor observes the silence closely, noting the rise in anxiety, so that she intervenes at the optimum time if no group member appears about to respond. A reflective or inquiring comment is often most facilitating. 'What do you think this silence is about?' In a structured group this comment might need more explanation for the style of intervention always depends on the group's aims and level of development.

Empowering the group

The conductor intervenes to facilitate the members' own activity but sometimes they resist this, wanting to establish a dependency culture, where only the conductor can help. Direct questions may be put to the conductor and even her silence constitutes a response. Answering questions may emphasise the members' dependence, or limit the contributions they can make. Often questions to the conductor seem so simple it appears peevish not to answer, and in some groups will drive members away. Into what is the conductor being drawn? A response such as 'I am happy to answer that but wonder if first it would be more useful if we could understand why you asked it', addresses the underlying process rather than the content. In a working group, within a short time, the question will have been answered or challenged by the members and the process of analysis begun.

The individual member must move from projecting his authority on to the conductor, consequentially ignoring, attacking or becoming dependent, to owning his authority and using it in his and the group's interest. The conductor can help or hinder this process. In this example (from Chapter 4) the conductor, who had taken the authority given to him by the group and used it in its interest, now allows it to be taken back from him, in keeping with the appropriate development of the group members. It may feel difficult for the conductor to give this authority up, but her role and the group's need of her steadily change.

> The session returns to an earlier theme with the news that the houses are sold. They are free to move... there are hints of unfinished business... Pauline's relationship has not developed and the group is disappointed... A heated exchange occurs about whether it is appropriate to discuss relationships outside the group. Those less involved in outside events want more interaction in the group... Others take this up, describing having used their energy to pass exams, write papers, do things they thought their families wanted. But it doesn't lead to acceptance by parents.

The conductor might have linked the desire to please parents to the desire to please him, but at this point a transference interpretation is not appropriate. The group moves onto a discussion about the relationships between men and women in the group with the men feeling that they are being manipulated. The conductor avoids emphasising his importance and the dependence on him.

Discussion

Gradually the group achieves a deepening level of verbal exploration. The conductor maintains her interest in several different levels (Chapter 4) in the group at the same time: the here and now, the relationships that emerge in the group, what is projected into other members and then integrated into the group. Material that is split off from the group and appears to be lost may be accessible to the conductor through her countertransference.

In a group there is an opportunity to experience and experiment with power in a new way. There is an equity between the group members in a stranger group. The members potentially offer protection and support to each other against the autocratic or unreasonable conductor so that she cannot easily use and abuse the power that has been projected into her. It is important to understand challenges to her authority within a developmental context.

Only through living with the group, exposing herself to its permeating currents, trying to understand what is happening, the relevance of each communication, will the conductor be able to decide on the nature and the timing of the various potential interventions she could make.

LEARNING POINTS

- The conductor thinks carefully about when it is necessary to intervene.
- Apart from boundary keeping, the conductor will mainly intervene when she sees that there is **resistance** to the free flow of communication.
- **Role suction, subgrouping** or **silence** may express resistance in the group.
- The conductor offers an **individual interpretation** when something has surfaced for a particular group member which the group cannot yet articulate.
- The conductor must be able to take up her **authority** and relinquish it to the group appropriately.

Some Types of Intervention in Group Analysis

The conductor also has to think about her style of intervention. Often she elucidates and clarifies what someone has said. This may emphasise or draw attention to something the group is ignoring. Occasionally she selects a topic for discussion, draws attention to something that is being glossed over or underlines something that will enter the group's memory to be addressed later. Reflecting on events in the group briefly or at length, drawing out an emerging pattern, brings the individual members to see themselves as part of the whole group.

> I was away, the following week only two came, and it seemed a very useful group; the next week when you two were away everyone else came. The mood seems very different today with everyone here. What can we make of these absences?

The conductor brings the background into focus so that it becomes the figure. She may make links between things people have said or not said, or explain links which are not being recognised. She may wonder why someone is being ignored, scapegoated or is the focus of projections. She may need to confront members. Her silence is also a communication.

Comments such as these aim to increase the integration of the group, increase the communication in the group and help the group to address issues. Group analysis does not draw a distinction between events in the group, and those occurring outside the boundary of the group. This is seen as a false dichotomy.

The conductor must talk back to the group in the language it understands, at its level. This is important even with seemingly simple comments such as 'Who else is feeling like this?' or 'What is this making others think of?' It is too easy to attempt to facilitate the group in a language or direction opposite to the one in which it is going.

Starting with the language the group is using, the **manifest content**, the conductor slowly helps the group understand the hidden meaning, the **latent content**. Once the member feels understood, or at least that his suffering is accepted, he will be ready to understand the unconscious meanings. The conductor moves from the **symptom** to the **underlying conflict**.

Some Theoretical Underpinnings of Group Therapy

We have been emphasising the importance of the group conductor focusing her interventions on the communication within the group, advocating certain sorts of interventions and suggesting that the conductor should be wary of others. This pragmatic understanding of her role draws on some ways of thinking about how group therapy can be a vehicle for psychological change.

BE WARY OF THESE INTERVENTIONS, THEY MAY BE DEFENSIVE

■ Classifying and categorising do little to increase the open communication tending to reassure and confirm difference.

■ Catching out and confrontations may have more to do with the conductor feeling powerful.

■ Transference interpretations and links to the past may sometimes be a way of escaping from the struggle of present feelings.

■ Plunging interpretations often link the present events in the group with the past addressing the associated primitive feelings. Given prematurely when the member is not ready to integrate the ideas they take both member and group away from the here and now. However, there are times when an individual or the whole group needs the conductor to make these or transference interpretations which can help the group to contain painful and difficult emotions.

Interpretation, analysis and insight: the relationship between group and individual therapy

The analytic and psychodynamic approaches to therapy and counselling believe that a combination of affect and insight enable a person to make psychological changes.

In individual therapy the agent of change is the relationship between two individuals, while in group therapy it is the membership of the group.

It may be the interaction between one member and another, with the conductor or with the group as a whole that is therapeutic: but in joining the group the individual gives up some of his autonomy, becoming part of a matrix of relationships. At times he communicates something on behalf of others as well as himself. He has a role beyond himself as a member of the group and as part of the whole group. (In the following two sections on group focal conflict theory and systems theory we will be looking at other ways of theorising this group experience.)

The group offers an opportunity to re-experience the emotional tension of past events in the here and now, in a different and it is to be hoped more responsive and empathic situation. The group member can integrate affects emerging in the present, responded to in a new way, with intellectual understanding and insight. Bringing together affect and insight enables change to occur in the psychic structure. This is the corrective emotional experience. It does not replace an old experience, but offers a new experience in the present.

Interpretation

In individual therapy the aim is to reach beneath the defence and anxiety to the hidden feeling and then trace this back to its origins in the past, usually parental relationships. Rarely is the whole interpretation offered at once, but it develops in the joint work of therapist and patient. There is a parallel to what happens in the group. The ideal time to interpret is when some or all of the group are on the edge of understanding something themselves. Interpretations made to the group lead to individual dynamics emerging. At such times work with an individual may be supported by the group.

There are times when the conductor should make an individual interpretation to a group member. This will usually be when the group does not appear able to address something which is happening for a group member, which the group conductor can see has reached the surface and needs to be made explicit. However, even when she has an individual interpretation *in her mind* she may express it in a different form. The conductor encouraged the group to take up Valerie's issues with her daughter in a different way (Chapter 4): had this not worked he might have considered an individual interpretation.

In this example from Chapter 4 working with the group leads to the emergence of an individual interpretation.

Foulkes (1975, p. 124) considers interpretation should address:

■ the interaction in the group
■ the way conflict is repeated in the group, the compulsion to repeat
■ childhood and past experiences that emerge in the group
■ current events occurring in the life of the member, outside and inside the group
■ boundary incidents occurring between the ongoing group and their ongoing life.

[The group is trying to come to terms with its ending.] There is a pause in the group, as if something needs to be said... Diana becomes aware of what she has not done. She speaks of a person who has committed suicide: then how the conductor's absence aroused feelings... anxiety... upset... about her father. She now avoids contact with the conductor... The group suggests she is expressing confused feelings others cannot yet put into words.

Through the conductor's absence, yet ongoing presence, Diana recognises a split-off aspect of her self which she fears to address. The conductor addresses her directly (see last box) using the opportunity for the individual, hoping the group will begin to explore at a new level.

Malan (1979, p. 80) in his classical text on individual therapy describes interpretation involving two triangles.

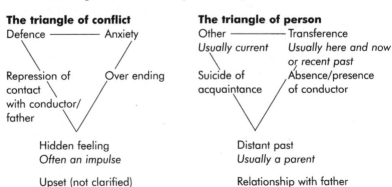

The triangle of conflict

Defence ———— Anxiety

Repression of   Over ending
contact
with conductor/
father

Hidden feeling
Often an impulse

Upset (not clarified)

The triangle of person

Other ———— Transference
Usually current   *Usually here and now
or recent past*
Suicide of   Absence/presence
acquaintance   of conductor

Distant past
Usually a parent

Relationship with father

In group-analytic therapy being aware of these different links for each person is important. Through observing the transference relationships in the here and now of the group, the recurrent patterns of interpersonal behaviour begin to have meaning. The need to avoid certain threatening situations in the past has led the individual to find a solution which leaves him cut off from an aspect of himself.

Group Focal Conflict Theory

Invited to discuss whatever is important to them, members associate, respond and resonate with each other. A group theme begins to emerge which has meaning for most of the members. Associated feelings, fears or wishes, give rise to anxieties; it is these conflictual ideas which form the group focal conflict. The group finds a solution, negotiates an agreement, to resolve the disturbing emotions (the reactive motive and the disturbing motive) associated with the theme. This reduces the members' fears or satisfies their wishes aroused by their resonance with the group theme. Resolution of the tensions (focal conflicts) that emerge in the group result in the development of the group culture (Whitaker and Lieberman, 1964).

Solutions tend to be of two types:

- **Enabling solutions** which reduce the anxiety while allowing the group to continue to explore the theme and its associated wish or impulse further: they enable the group to continue to develop.
- **Restrictive solutions** which reduce the group's anxiety by providing a solution which addresses the group's fear or guilt about the theme, but fails to address the unconscious wish or impulse.

Clinical example

The group struggles with its anxieties at the first meeting, compounded by the wobbly boundaries. It seems to be making connections between the conductor's initial failure and previous examples of being let down. Group members do not mention their anxieties about this strange new group but move from self-revelatory stories about breaches of confidentiality (indicating fears about the safety of this group) to suggesting that the group must conform to certain standards of political correctness.

The conductor intervenes to stop what he sees as a restrictive solution; namely that the group should be 'politically correct', as a way of trying to provide a solution to the problems posed by its dark side, the shadow, of the group being exposed.

A diagrammatic version of what we have just described.

Group theme
Trust in the group

Group focal conflict

Reactive motive
Fear or guilt
Be exposed in an unsupportive
structure

Disturbing motive
Wish or impulse
Wish for trust and a
reliable structure

Solution
*Enables the group to cope with the fear but does not address
the disturbing motive*
Adopt strict rules of conduct from society; political correctness

The **group culture**, which may be restrictive or enabling, develops in response to the different solutions agreed by the group. Intervening to support the development of enabling solutions increases the ability of the group to address disturbing issues and explore new understandings. It involves maintaining an optimum anxiety level where defensive solutions do not emerge. Enabling solutions are not always good and their restrictive counterparts bad: early in the group in Chapter 4, the conductor recognises that the group's retreat to talking about a problem outside itself may be a restrictive solution which it needs to lower the tension in the group at that point.

The Dynamics of Group and Individual Systems

'Patrolling the Boundary' and the Summary in Chapter 5 outline aspects of systems theory. The group, like all living organisms, is a system interacting with its environment. Exchange across the boundary is necessary for a system to continue to survive. Healthy systems have selective, semi-permeable boundaries and are able to integrate new information, or close their boundaries if the system's survival is threatened. New energy enters the group; there is a disturbance to the equilibrium as people cross the boundary and there is a disclosure or expression of feeling. Challenges to the status quo of the group result in the reinforcing of the previous structure, often by the boundary becoming less permeable (new information being excluded), or a new equilibrium emerging that incorporates the new information.

> The conductor of the group in Chapter 4 announced that he would be away for a session, expecting the group to meet without him. The group could have explored its feelings about having no conductor, but it appointed an informal leader from the group, re-establishing the status quo, and closing the boundary to possible new information and further development of the system (group). The conductor could understand why the woman who 'led' the group might have chosen to do so in terms of her own history, but it was clear that this was a group issue since all had allowed her to take up her position.

Applying general systems theory to group psychotherapy, Agazarian and Peters (1981) develop the idea that sub-systems within a larger system are hierarchically related and each reflects aspects of the other (isomorphy). They observe a group from four perspectives:

- the person perspective
- member role perspective
- group role perspective
- group-as-a-whole perspective.

These perspectives have a developmental sequence. The member joins as an individual, and begins to interact with the others in the group. He moves across a boundary to become part of another system, the group, when he interacts with others as a member of part or all the group. This move across the boundary is a turning point involving a major change for some people. He is then functioning within two systems. Further development, another turning point, occurs as the member becomes part of the group as a whole, realising he is influenced by and influences this system. Moving into the group role system may well be a corrective emotional experience as the member finds himself performing a role acting for the group or containing emotions or conflict. Therapy involves the individual being increasingly free to move into and out of these different systems. This is another way of describing the aim of increasing the range and expression of communication.

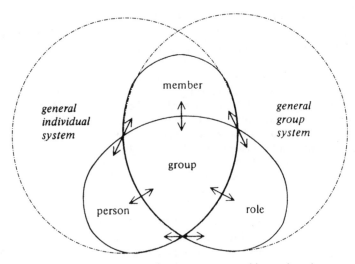

The arrows represent outputs from one system and inputs into the next.
These input/output relationships exist between four co-existing systems.
(Agazarian and Peters, 1981, p. 44)

Figure 6.1   Relationships between the systems of person, member,
role and group

Joan (see Chapter 4) shows these progressive moves in her membership
of the group: having refused to join with the rest of the group in telling
others her name, staying in the person perspective, she wears a name
badge and moves into member role. She joins with others in expressing
resentment at the move as part of the group as a whole. Likewise she acts
for the group as a whole as well as in member role when she pushes the
group into allowing her to be the conductor when he is absent. She takes
a group role perspective when arguing for the group to continue, speaks
for one group as a whole.

In a mature group the conductor could point out to one member that he
was expressing all the anger about a break, when everyone else seemed
pleased. Clarification of the group role would enable him to draw in the
other members to express their resentment, which can only happen
because he is acting for the group system. If there was no boundary
around him and the others, he would be a scapegoat, and such an intervention would push him further out of the group, as could easily have
happened to Kingston in the first session.

Therapeutic activity can only occur once the boundaries are clearly
established and the group cannot function at a higher level until these

fundamental issues are resolved. When boundary issues are addressed, energy no longer leaks out of the group and is thus more available within the group to be used in the interests of both individuals and the group. Agazarian and Peters (1981) propose a hierarchy of interventions, the conductor first addressing boundary issues involving destructive group roles (for example scapegoating), then absences, before addressing boundary issues contained within the group. Only then does the conductor address the integrative processes of the group, deepening and broadening the group's therapeutic activity for the whole group, then addressing subgroups and finally individual members.

The model shows how important it is to draw people and their energy into the system ('group') at the beginning of a session, as Foulkes (1964) wrote 35 years earlier, describing the need for the conductor often to be active in the new group and at the beginning of each session. It also offers the conductor opportunities to see when energy or affects are not being contained within the boundaries of the group, for example when the group in Chapter 4 becomes involved with one of their members establishing a relationship outside of the group.

The Conductor Intervenes: An Overview

The conductor cannot maintain an empathic responsiveness with each individual member of the group at all times. Her focus moves from one figure to another as they emerge from the ground of the group matrix. If change only occurs through each individual having the sense of being personally psychologically held and empathically understood, then the conductor has an impossible task. Empathic responsiveness is provided by the society of the group, the individuals in it, as well as by the conductor. To establish the therapeutic alliance and the necessary conditions for therapy, the conductor must create the group where all members are actively involved, interacting with each other, associating silently or giving voice to the resonance aroused in them. This is the first aim of the conductor. It is through being part of the group, resonating herself to the content and process of the group and using her countertransference response to guide her interventions, that the conductor can respond to the need which each individual has to be reflected and recognised in the group.

The theories and concepts given in this chapter guide and inform her in this task, but spontaneous interactions between the members involve the conductor being able to use her own spontaneity in the interests of the group. Like the group members she has to be open to unconscious processes and her spontaneity while thinking within a defined structure.

Despite spending so much time creating, maintaining and developing the group, the conductor must also have a sense of each individual. She must be aware of them as individuals interacting in the group, struggling to use it for their own gain. She should understand the recurrent solutions each person uses in response to stress, watching for them to emerge in the group, in interaction with others, aware this has parallels to their lives outside. The group exists for the benefit of the individual members, yet they can only benefit by giving up aspects of themselves to the group. She must foster an understanding of the group as an entity that is more than the individuals, that is, 'different from the sum of its parts' (Lewin, 1951, p. 146).

7
Differences in Groups: Heterogeneity and Homogeneity

Introduction

We often think about a group of people in terms of what they have in common; their differences, however, can also be important, especially those with an obvious social significance. In a therapy group we have to go beyond a legalistic or politically correct way of looking at racial, gender and other differences. We have looked in detail at the ways in which the group conductor strives to make the group a safe space where a wide variety of feelings can be explored without being enacted. Group members also need to be able to explore their differences in the knowledge that that there will be no active reprisals. The group conductor must develop her own personal awareness to make full use of her countertransference just as she does in other emotionally significant areas. She will, for example, need to explore her own responses to disability, and also be clear about how the group's boundaries will make exploration of this theme safe. Looking at the differences between people can be a difficult and painful process; it is important to understand the origin of such difficulties. It is only through looking at what actually happens in groups that the necessity of confronting differences becomes apparent.

As part of this discussion we will look at the reasons for sometimes selecting therapy groups in which all members share a common problem, attribute or situation, such as a group for people with alcohol problems, a group for Asian mothers or for people with eating disorders. We will discuss how such homogeneous groups can be helpful and how, even in these groups, the conductor needs to be aware of the differences between the group members.

The Psychology of Difference

What makes difference difficult?

Being in a group highlights the conflicts that everyone has about being the same and being different. A person often wants to be part of a group so that she can be with other similar people and can feel a sense of warm togetherness. Yalom (1995) suggested recognition of similarity (universality) with others is one of the most important factors in group therapy. However, the experience of similarity and sharing may make you lose your sense of yourself and feel too merged into the others. Regaining your sense of individuality can be a discomforting process as you become aware of differences between you and other group members, which may make you feel jealous, deprived, snobbish, competitive or isolated.

Let us take an example from daily life: George is poring over brochures trying to decide whether to go on a skiing holiday. Apart from the practical considerations such as the timing, the cost, the snow and the ski-lift, he is thinking about the group. He likes the idea of having companions. The brochure seems to be aimed at people like him, who do not want a run-of-the-mill holiday. He can imagine fitting into this group of people, getting to know them on the journey out and developing a convivial atmosphere. He has almost decided to book his holiday when he is beset by other thoughts and images; what if he finds it hard to like some of the other people? Perhaps they will want to go to after-ski venues which George would find distasteful and he would feel compelled to join them. He begins to imagine himself swept up in a group desire which will overwhelm his individuality and which he will be unable to resist.

Looking at George's dilemma about this putative skiing group we can see how they illustrate the basic forces of attraction and repulsion in groups. Initially, George liked the idea of being part of a group with shared aspirations; implicit in this was probably some covert assumptions about age, class, education and possibly ethnicity.

George begins to have doubts for two apparently contradictory reasons. He worries about feeling negative towards people in the group who are different from him. He is also afraid that the pressure to be similar will make him lose his identity and sweep him up in a current of conformity. Paradoxically, his fear of being merged or submerged may lead him to define himself as different, in opposition to others to whom he attributes negative qualities.

If George had started to analyse his responses, he might have surmised that he was fearful of being envious and competitive towards other members of the party. Perhaps he had fantasies of developing a relationship with one of the women in the party, which might result in his pushing out other men or being ousted by another man himself. These feelings in turn might have strong resonances with George's own family experience. Since George is only planning a holiday he may not want to think about himself in this way, but in a therapy group whose purpose is to understand what people feel about each other, these differences need to be explored, for underlying the feelings are some basic psychological and social dimensions of experience.

The roots of the difficulties

As we saw in Chapter 2, in early infancy the baby has little sense of the difference between himself and the mother (or carer). Being part of someone else (as the baby was in the womb) can give a wonderful sense of safety and belonging. The recognition that he is not part of his mother is learned slowly and painfully, as he discovers that she can withdraw from him and his needs. How this is learned may be a crucial determinant of the person's capacity to have a full emotional life. Can the baby learn that the mother is separate and different, feel loss and anger and yet still be able to feel closeness and love for the mother? Can the baby learn to mobilise the anger in ways which allow for him to develop creatively or is the anger harnessed to destructive or self-destructive ends?

This process is not an all or nothing affair. For the majority of people, the internal world consists of various aspects of the self being represented in what Bollas (1993, p. 197) describes as a **parliamentary order**, with different aspects jostling to be heard and processed. Bollas suggests that when things are not too pressured, all goes well and the plurality and ambivalence of the world and relationships can be accepted within the individual. However, when there is strong psychic pressure, the processing ceases and instead different parts of the self are projected out into other objects. This has two important consequences; others are invested with the bad qualities which the individual can no longer bear to keep inside and the individual himself feels depleted. Those designated as *other,* who are different, can easily be seen as bad, while *I* remain good. Bollas describes this as the origin of what he terms the **fascist state of mind**.

The unconscious attempts to resolve the painful aspects of difference and differentiating are reinforced within society by the way in which social splits acquire a history of antagonism and power differentials, often leading to exploitation of one group by another and the abuse of power. In other words, within society we have categories of people who become psychological dumping grounds for others. An obvious example of this is racism where white people split off negative aspects of themselves which are projected into black people, whom they then attack for *being black*. This process is intensified for both black and white people by the history of colonialism and imperialism, including the enslavement of black people by whites (Dalal, 1997). What this extreme (although not unusual) example reiterates is that each individual is formed not only by the interactions between himself and his family, but also by the social and historical context within which he lives.

The feeling which one person has towards another is given additional meaning by the social nature of the relationship between the two. The interaction between an Indian woman working in the post office and her white working-class customer, who is upset because her new benefit book has not arrived, is influenced for both by the history of colonialism and imperialism in the past. It is further affected by common forms of social projection which may allow either of the two people involved to think that somehow the Asian postwoman is responsible for the white customer's plight. Similarly some of George's fears about the skiing holiday may be connected to his self-image as a white, educated, middle-class man, who is afraid his masculinity will be threatened by seemingly stronger and sexier working-class men. George's sense of identity may be maintained by excluding certain attributes. He may then split them off into people from *other* groups, such as more powerful middle-class people, women or working-class men.

These differences are often reinforced by imbalances of social power which may be at variance with the individual's fantasies. Thus the white working-class customer has the fantasy that she is being deprived by the Indian postwoman. Remembering Bollas' account of the development of the fascist state of mind (which might be in any of us) the customer is feeling deprived, devalued, angry and lacking in self-esteem. She needs someone to blame; she wants to focus her anger on someone whom she perceives as hurting her. She also wants to do something with the bad feelings she has about herself and the part she may unconsciously believe that she has played in creating her own deprived circumstances. Mentally she places both the power and her badness inside the postwoman. She then feels even more depleted because she has lost both her benefit book and her internal power.

Yet historically, the relationship is based on the events which led the Indian postwoman to become a resident of the UK and the white working-class customer to be living on state benefit. Perhaps both had experienced harassment on the streets or in their homes. George also feels potentially at the mercy of all the imagined members of his skiing trip.

These complex interrelationships are played out in a therapy group which can develop understanding for all the members if the social aspects and the issues of subjugation and domination are taken up.

LEARNING POINTS

- Group conductors need to look at their own responses to socially significant differences in the same way as they need to be as aware as possible of other aspects of their emotional life.
- Within a group the individual wants to be like the other group members and at the same time fears that his own identity may be submerged by the group. In this environment inner conflict may be expressed in terms of hatred of another socially disadvantaged subgroup.
- The origins of the hatred of other social groups lie both in primitive psychological mechanisms and in the social and political context.

Working with Differences in Groups

Giving the subject a voice

A group may intensify the degree of splitting and projection between members while also offering the possibility of examining the projections and helping individuals to re-own their split-off parts. Where this involves socially charged differences, it is particularly important for the group conductor to acknowledge them and enable them to be voiced, both within herself and in the group. Blackwell (1994, p. 202) argues that the maxim that the conductor should follow where the group leads does not mean that the conductor should avoid making interpretations about rivalry, dependency or sexuality if these are not explicitly mentioned in the group. Similarly she should have her antennae tuned to issues of colonialism and racism (and other relevant social and historical issues) even if these are not overtly spoken about. The group conductor needs to be attuned to the **social unconscious**.

CASE EXAMPLE

In an ongoing therapy group, a new member was introduced. In the first session there was a very light and warm atmosphere. The discussion was about games which group members had played with their brothers and sisters. The new member joined in saying she was the middle one of three children, had always felt left out being neither special as the eldest, nor the baby of the family. Another group member identified with this saying she would never have three children.

The group conductor felt as if she was invisible, was enraged and bursting to say something. She could not tolerate the light tone in contrast with her state of mind. Reminding herself to think about her countertransference, she restrained herself from speaking and allowed her mind to wander. How could she feel so upset about being ignored by the group when they had a new member in a wheelchair, who was so obviously disadvantaged? The group conductor felt helpless and began to picture herself with her leg in plaster and a pair of crutches resting on the chair. Her leg was uncomfortable but the rest of her body relaxed. As she experienced the release of tension, she saw herself sitting next to the new group member slightly separated from the rest of the group. As long as she too was suffering from a disability she could be close to the new person and not feel guilty. She had as much right as anyone else to speak. Were the other able-bodied group members trying to find a way of identifying with the woman in the wheelchair in order to escape from their discomfort at the disability?

The group conductor said that the group was behaving as if they were all suffering from the disability of being blind and unable to see the new member in the wheelchair. She suggested that this allowed the whole group to be the same in their blindness, perpetuating the family myth that all children are treated the same and loved equally. One or two group members were relieved and able to say that they hadn't known how to react when the new member arrived in a wheelchair. They were afraid of upsetting her. The new member was able to say that she had expected them to be dismayed and disappointed that someone like her was joining the group. The group conductor no longer felt so angry and excluded but was aware of the hurt and pain in the room.

In this session, the group members were denying their feelings towards the newcomer. They felt paralysed (or as the conductor put it, blinded) by the complexity of their ambivalent and guilty feelings. They were jealous of the new baby who, with her disability, might take more of mother's attention. They were frightened of their negative and hostile feelings towards the disabled woman, perhaps even feeling pleased that they were not in the wheelchair. They also had more conventional responses such as pity, sympathy and even curiosity about a physically vulnerable person whom they did not want to hurt. Some of them were aware of the unwelcome attention she might receive in her daily life as well as the practical difficulties. They did not want to appear prejudiced so they tried to resolve their conflicting feelings by not noticing.

The new group member also used her well-established protective shell prior to the group conductor's intervention. She colluded with the denial of her difference when she spoke about her lack of specialness in her family. She repressed her rage about her condition and other people's incapacity to respond appropriately, drawing on her own social conditioning as a person who has to cope with both the social stigma and the practical problems associated with her condition.

The group conductor based her intervention on her countertransference, and initiated a situation in which they could begin to work on the unconscious meanings of disability for them as individuals and as a group.

The crucial first step is for the group to begin to speak about the taboo topic. As long as this does not happen, the whole group may be stuck and neither those members who belong to the minority grouping nor the rest of the group will have a full voice. Although there may be common issues of social power, and common processes of splitting and projection, the specific forms of fantasy, conflict and silence vary with the particularity of every difference. We have deliberately chosen examples from a range of social differences to encourage readers to explore their own experience as widely as possible.

Both Rippa (1994) and Blackwell (1994) describe situations where once the *secret* about the oppressed group members is spoken about it enables those members to participate much more fully in the group, bringing in personal material. Rippa describes how the only Arab member in an otherwise Jewish group in Israel at the time of the Gulf War was enabled 'to work out personal issues that he could not believe that he could bring up in a training group. His speech changed and his voice became louder and clearer.' Interestingly enough, the Arab member identified himself rather than being helped by the group conductors. Rippa explains that: 'The heightened emotional climate of the war was the trigger', thus suggesting that under normal circumstances the conductors would have had to be more active in encouraging the group to speak about the difference.

Blackwell writes about another training group, in England, which had three black and five white members. It was only through a series of steps taken by the white group conductor that the black members were eventually able to 'recount their almost daily experience of racism' (1994, p. 199). He began by acknowledging that it might be difficult for one of the black group members to be in a group where English jokes were told which he could not follow. Then he pointed out that something strange was happening in a group which decided to define an Irish group member as not being an immigrant, thus implicitly saying that only black members were immigrants. This enabled the black members to join the group in a different way. 'They found a greater freedom to talk about their families and culture which could be recognised by the other group members as being significantly different from white English family and community life' (p. 200).

These examples show how vital it is to speak about the *awkward* social differences in a group. They also raise two important questions: how can such issues be explored in a group when the minority consists of one? Is it possible to go beyond speaking about the difference, to a deeper level of exploring it within a heterogeneous group? Answering these questions will lead on to the discussion of the value and limitations of homogeneous groups.

Group composition and social factors

Chapter 3 looked at the way in which a group is selected, trying to ensure that no group member is noticeably isolated from the start. These considerations also apply to the issues discussed in this chapter. We have seen how the majority group may try to protect itself and the lone individual by denying any difference, an inverted form of scapegoating, or the individual may actually be scapegoated in more or less subtle ways.

When the differences are acknowledged, the majority may demand that the isolate take up the role of spokesperson for her particular grouping; for example, explaining her experience as a black woman. This locates difference in blackness as if the experience of being white does not require discussion. If she challenges this, refusing to take on the role of group educator, she risks alienating other group members and may need the conductor's support. Alternatively, if she wants to work out her personal problems, she may decide to keep quiet and as Blackwell describes it, take on 'the status of honorary white'. Blackwell comments: 'The fact that a whole dimension of their experience is ignored may not be a small price to pay, but at least it is a price they are used to paying' (1994, p. 204).

In practical terms, where a service allows for selection, it is most effective to try to ensure that there are no isolated group members. A mixed-race group works best when there are at least three members of each subgroup. A pair can feel both isolated and forced into an unchosen relationship. However, often the choice is between being the only person with, for instance, a disability or no therapy at all. Here several factors have to be considered. First, it will be up to the group conductor to maintain her awareness of how disability/able-bodiedness may affect what happens in the group, to contain the feelings and to work with them, bearing in mind the power differential. She will have to judge, and discuss in supervision, how much of this she should make explicit and how much the whole group will suffer if differences are denied. Much of this will depend on the individual's and the group's particular capacities and defences.

The conductor will have to think about whether this particular person has enough ego-strength and motivation to gain something from the group, in spite of the inevitable blunderings which will take place, and of the possibly insufficient exploration of certain aspects of her experience.

The concerns of a homosexual joining the group may be different from those of a black person or a person with a disability. The black person has always been black, whereas the homosexual may have spent part of his life identifying himself as a heterosexual or passing as such. Moreover he may see homosexuality as a chosen rather than a received identity. A woman who has developed a disability only in adult life will be dealing with different issues from the one who was born blind. Any group member has the potential to become disabled or to discover their homosexual desires whereas a white person cannot become black, but might choose a black partner and have a black child. This has implications for the dynamics of difference and informs the discussion about homogeneous groups.

Beyond the first step

Making the social difference visible in the group opens the horizon out for all the members, raising the question of how far a mixed or heterogeneous group can go in understanding each other's underlying experiences. Not to go further will diminish the value of the group to both the less and the more powerful subgroupings. For some it may be intolerable and they will leave.

Returning to the example of the group with one disabled member, all the members will constantly be reminded by her presence in the group, of how it is to live in a predominantly able-bodied society. Her presence may highlight feelings in other group members about dependency and independence, damaging and being damaged, and self-image, for example. The challenge is to unpack these experiences without reinforcing them through making the woman in the wheelchair listen to more expressions of rejection, patronising remarks or disgust.

We do not want to underestimate what is involved in addressing these issues, nor do we think that the group-analytic approach has easy answers. What we can do is show how thinking about our experience in this work can help the group conductor and the group to develop a greater capacity to work with all group members.

The next example shows how one white group conductor and his mixed-race group learned slowly and painfully to begin a dialogue; the dialogue was about how it felt to be black, to experience racism and its psychological effects, and how it felt to be white and to begin to really hear this and acknowledge the complicity of white people who did not consciously wish to be racist.

CASE EXAMPLE

The therapy group had three black and four white members. Paula, a black group member, found the group distressing and feared it jeopardised her relationships at home and at work. Paula found her distress as unacceptable as the dreadful smell which she believed emanated from her. Group members had told Paula that she did not smell and had interpreted it as a way of expressing how bad she felt about herself. June, a white woman, told Paula that she had found expressing her feelings helpful although other group members agreed that it could be disruptive to relationships outside the group. While Paula was talking about herself, Shirley (a white woman) said that she urgently needed to talk about something in the group. Paula apologised and there was no further discussion of the incident. Soon after Paula announced that she was too distressed to continue in the group.

The group conductor thought that he had been wrong to choose Paula for a once-weekly group, rather than thinking about the group dynamics preceding Paula's departure. When he presented the group to a case discussion seminar he was amazed to find that the black and white members of the seminar were soon locked into a polarised argument. The black therapists felt that the conductor had not taken Paula's needs seriously or been aware of how the other black group members felt when Paula became so distressed and left the group. The group conductor felt crushed, as if his expertise in group therapy was being devalued. As an Irish man, he had seen himself as a fellow immigrant to England, having a special empathy with black people. Now he was virtually being accused of being a racist; and they didn't seem to be concerned with all the group members, only the black ones. Was he being told that black people needed protecting from white therapists like himself?

Meanwhile, the black therapists were despairing. They thought the white group conductor had not even attempted to understand what might be happening for the black people in his group. They felt angry and protective. They wondered whether it would not be best to have all the black patients seen by black therapists.

While the therapy group had evicted or lost Paula, the case discussion group was polarising between black and white members. The two convenors of the case discussion suggested that this polarisation needed to be understood. They reminded the discussants that talking about racial issues was bound to be stormy because it was about racism; something which affected even the most determinedly anti-racist person. This reassured the black discussants that their viewpoint would be heard and also calmed the white participants as they felt less personally accused and guilty.

Eventually they developed an account of the group process which suggested that neither the group conductor nor the group members had been able to think about how Paula's blackness might have influenced what happened in the group. While reassuring Paula that she did not smell bad and trying to interpret her symptom, no one had related it to her feelings about being black. They did not acknowledge that the way black people are often labelled as dirty in this society might have affected Paula's feelings about herself. The group would have had to face racism just as the case discussion group had done. For Paula to have got rid of her fear of smelling, some of the other unsavoury feelings would have had to be shared around the group.

Unconsciously the group conductor had been afraid of a polarised conflict between black and white people in his therapy group; in the case discussion what he feared happened. The ugliest feelings were expressed: black and white people polarised, but as a result they communicated. There was no need for a scapegoat. Subsequently in the group the conductor became more confident in encouraging dialogue between white and black members.

CASE EXAMPLE

A few months later June (a white group member) said that in her experience all black men are bastards. There was a silence; the group conductor wondered what to do and wished she hadn't said it. He could feel the intense discomfort in the room. Usually he waited to see how the group would respond to a provocative statement but he realised that this would allow the group to become a place in which there was no possibility of addressing racism. If he said nothing the group would become unsafe for black members and, in a different way, for white ones too. If he challenged June, she would become entrenched, angry that her suffering was always minimised while others were given special treatment. The other group members would be able to maintain their positions as never having unpleasant thoughts or feelings like June's.

Eventually he broke the silence saying that it wasn't acceptable to make generalisations about black men (or any other types) in the group but perhaps June wanted to talk about what was behind the statement. June was furious with the group conductor. She had been encouraged to speak freely in the group and now she was told to shut up; the group conductor favoured the black members and the young women. He wanted to ingratiate himself with them. In an emotional outburst she told the group how no one had loved her, she felt worthless and as the eldest of a huge family her needs were never noticed. Hugh said it was strange that she didn't express more resentment to the group family as she had to share with them too. Why was she so busy talking about black men in general rather than what she felt about particular black people in the group?

Following this session June was absent; she rang to say she was ill. On her return she was shaky and still angry with the group conductor. Meanwhile the group, without June, had had a chance to talk through what had happened and to understand both how June displaced her anger onto black people and how the more overtly liberal members used June as a mouthpiece. June expressed her deprivation within the group at being offered a paltry hour and a half a week when she needed at least twice-weekly groups, if not more. Once June had been challenged about venting her feelings on anonymous black men outside the group, but invited to explore those very feelings within the group, she was able to recognise and express her envy of the black women in the group who, as she saw it, got more attention than she did. She began to connect the group and her family understanding her resentment of the group conductor/parent who would not give her special attention. Other group members identified with the way June displaced her feelings about the pain and abuse of her own childhood onto 'black men out there' rather than working with the feelings aroused by actual individuals within the group. Other white group members were able to recognise that they wanted to distance themselves from June to avoid their taboo racist feelings. They acknowledged how difficult it is to think about what black people had to put up with or to feel implicated in racism. Paul, one of the white men, remembered that he had ignored what Doreen (the oldest black woman in the group) was saying, had changed the subject and no one had stopped him.

'Even our holier than thou group conductor has dirty hands in this matter.'

General laughter followed. This enabled Anita, the youngest black woman, to talk about how it had felt to be shouted at in the playground just because you were black. The black women moved on to discuss how they were treated in public places.

White and black people are talking about their different experiences in a group and can tolerate listening to each other. The group conductor had learned that he needed to make the group safe for discussion to take place between black and white group members just as he was responsible for other aspects of the group's safety. He realised that trying to smooth over the differences might lead to another black person leaving the group or a reduced level of participation among the black members. He also recognised that by allowing June and other white members to perpetuate their displacements onto black people they too would not be gaining all they could from the group. He had gained courage from surviving the conflict in the case discussion group and was able to intervene in a direct way. He deliberately drew a firm boundary against the acceptance of racist talk while making it clear to all group members that he was interested in what lay behind such statements, even if it was profoundly disturbing.

We have looked at the importance, the potential and the difficulties in working with social differences in groups, tried to understand some of the underlying dynamics and thought about how the group conductor can intervene. We have stressed the importance of the group conductor working on her own **social unconscious**, recognising that aspect of self-knowledge has been underdeveloped in training until recently.

However, groups which are structured around an issue or a quality shared by all the group members are also valuable, and we now turn to them.

LEARNING POINTS

- Speaking about the differences in a group, rather than pretending they are not there, is an essential first step. The conductor may have to do this if the group members seem unable to.

- Once the differences in the group are explicit it can be particularly enabling for the more *oppressed* group members to make use of the group. It is also freeing for the whole group.
- When group members are being selected it is important to pay attention to issues such as race, sexual orientation, disability or age and include more than two members from a particular social grouping.
- When this is impossible the conductor will think with the potential isolate about whether he will be able to make use of the group and how the conductor can best facilitate him.
- In selection and in the work of the group it is important to recognise that the meaning of, for example, homosexuality for the individual will be different from the meaning of, for example, being black.
- Once a group does begin to explore unconscious social issues the conductor will receive powerful projections which need to be taken to supervision for discussion.
- A supervision group can mirror the dynamics of a therapy group and if this is understood provides a valuable vehicle for learning.
- It is helpful for everyone concerned to be reminded that, within an historically racist society (such as the UK), all members of that society will be affected even where their conscious beliefs are strongly anti-racist. (The same goes for other issues such as homosexuality or social class.)

Homogeneous Groups

Assumptions about homogeneous groups

In everyday life a person who is struggling with a new and difficult experience may be helped by talking to others in a similar position. A new mother at the baby clinic chats to others as she is waiting to see the nurse and doctor. She discovers that other mothers have felt at the end of their tether after sleepless nights, have found breast feeding painful and difficult, or have felt guilty at changing over to bottle feeding. A man who has recently lost his job finds it reassuring to talk to others in a similar position and to recognise that he was not dismissed for being an inadequate worker.

A professional working with clients or patients may draw similar conclusions, thinking it would help them to talk to each other. A GP, who sees several unemployed male patients with minor physical symptoms and depression associated with loss of jobs, may think they would benefit from talking to each other. A social worker notices that a significant number of her adult women clients have been sexually abused in childhood; it might help them to talk together in a group. A counsellor working with the shocked victims of a ferry disaster notices such similarities between what is being said that he thinks the counselling should be re-organised into groups.

Hudson (1990) suggests that there are three main reasons for conducting homogeneous groups. Some people need different treatment because of their vulnerability and thus could not be expected to join a mixed group. This might be true for a schizophrenic patient and also for those addicted to alcohol or other drugs. Some need the presence of those who have shared a similar experience to transform it from something unthinkable to something which can be thought about, integrated into their personality and thus be made more manageable. This might apply to disaster survivors. Others need a homogeneous group to validate a particular area of experience which might otherwise be drowned out in a heterogeneous group. This might apply to all those sharing a particular social identity such as an ethnic minority group or lesbians.

We will show how all of these factors are present to varying degrees in homogeneous groups and can make them a valuable form of treatment, and at times, the treatment of choice.

CATEGORIES OF HOMOGENEOUS GROUPS

- Groups for people suffering loss or bereavement, for example children who have lost a parent, widows, recently disabled people.
- Groups for people who share a problem such as eating disorders, people who abuse alcohol or other drugs, compulsive gamblers or have a serious illness.
- Groups for people who are having difficulties in a shared phase of life, for example parents' groups, students' groups, groups for the elderly.
- Groups for people who have been victims of abuse or disasters, for example children or adults who have been raped or sexually abused, people who have been tortured, those who have suffered accidental or natural disasters.
- Groups for the perpetrators of various forms of abuse and crime.
- Groups for people sharing a particular social identity chosen or not, for example working-class people, rich people, black people, other ethnic groupings, lesbians or gay men.
- Groups for those diagnosed as having similar psychological or psychiatric problems, for example schizophrenics, agoraphobics, obsessional people.

Beyond common sense

Often homogeneous groups are seen as being akin to self-help and the group conductor thinks that the group-analytic approach which she applies for other groups is irrelevant. We have argued that a group-analytic way of thinking can help groups to be far more effective but applying it to homogeneous groups requires a different way of working.

The value of homogeneous groups for sharing similar experiences has been recognised. 'Survivors of the same experience provide support and containment by virtue of their shared experience' (Garland, 1991).

A group for compulsive eaters illustrates how the work goes beyond simple sharing and encouragement. Initially the eight women in the group find relief in sharing the private difficulties they have had for years in trying to control what they experience as an obsession with food, and the terrible associated feelings about their bodies. Finding that others in the group lead similar *double lives* breaks the isolation. It also lessens feelings of shame and abnormality. This can encourage a woman to look behind her apparently self-destructive behaviour and discover its meaning.

A woman who cannot begin to translate her unwanted behaviour and preoccupation with food into emotional terms may need to have her experience validated and understood *within its own language* before she is ready to enter the arena of the heterogeneous therapy group where the work of translating her behaviour into communication with others can be developed. As well as the need for a group which can share the metaphorical meaning of food, there may also be social factors at work. Not having control around food has a profound social stigma attached to it and the preoccupation with body image and staying slim are so prevalent that it may be difficult to create an environment in which such social attitudes can be temporarily held at bay so that initial work can be done. The homogeneous group can provide this setting before a woman is ready for the more robust heterogeneous group setting.

A study of self-help groups for compulsive eaters showed the difficulties homogeneous groups face in taking their members beyond the stage of sharing (Parry Crooke, 1980). Initially, these groups functioned well without group facilitators and members found them helpful and harmonious. After about six months the groups ran into difficulties and asked for professional support. What emerged at this stage was that the groups began to move on from their original preoccupation with food and fat and were beginning to look at the underlying meaning of their symptoms. Some group members were ready for this while others were not. They found it difficult to look at their differences and work through the group conflicts.

The paradox of homogeneous groups

The similarity of homogeneous group members offers each person a mirroring of her experience which can be validating and containing. At the same time, a group matrix is developing, the painful underlying feelings are being intensified and forced to the surface. The group conductor enables the group members to communicate with each other and ensure that confrontation happens in a way which does not fragment the group. As the group moves from the supportive aspects of sharing into the more frightening areas of transition and change, the group conductor enables members to see their differences within the shared meaning of what is happening in the group.

The conductor will use her transference and countertransference as she would in a heterogeneous group, but she will be translating them in terms of the shared symptom, problem or life situation. The theme is thought about group analytically.

Writing about a group for women who had been sexually abused in childhood, Rosenfeld and Dawson (1993) noted: 'It emerged from our experience and from the literature that the notion of the couple has special significance for this group.' The women's experience of coming between the parental couple meant that it was particularly important for the co-therapists to establish themselves as a working couple from the start, by ensuring that both met with each woman before the group began. One woman began to see one of the therapists, in the transference, as her mother who did not believe her or protect her from her abusing father. When the women in the group began to talk about feeling trapped in the circle this was related to the feeling of being pinned down by the abuser during the sexual act. At times the negative transference to the therapists was so strong that the women could only 'relate to the other group members, sharing their experiences and emotions with each other, knowing that they would be understood. They took from each other in a way that they could not from us.' The group conductors saw each of these incidents as having meaning within the framework of a family within which abuse had taken place.

Groups for people with a particular symptom require the therapist to think about what is happening in the group using the metaphoric language of the symptom. In Chapter 1 we saw how one member of a group for agoraphobia expressed part of the shared symptomatology of the whole group. Bulimic women recognise, through their group, that bingeing and vomiting is a metaphor for the way in which they lead their lives without digesting their own experience. A group of compulsive eaters discovers how the group reflects the emotional conflicts which they try to avoid or bury in being fat and preoccupied with food. Once the group members begin to translate their symptoms into words and understand how they are expressed in the relationships with each other, they may be ready to move on to therapy groups where the differences between members are immediately apparent. There they will be able to focus on new learning about themselves rather than reinforcing the definition of themselves as abused, bulimic or compulsive eater. It is important to limit the time spent in a homogeneous group so that each person's identity is able to develop beyond being defined by a symptom or a trauma.

Life cycle groups

Groups for people at particular stages of the life cycle differ in that often group members may range from people who have never seen themselves as having emotional difficulties to those with psychiatric histories. What they share is the theme of the particular transition; how they respond will be largely determined by their own past experience, their present circumstances and state of mind. Often such groups may focus on the meaning of the shared experience and how it manifests itself in the group, leaving it up to the individuals to make sense of what this means to them personally. In this respect such groups have affinities with those described in Chapter 8.

Let us look at two contrasting examples.

CASE EXAMPLE

In an experiential group for students on a counselling course the group offers students a chance to understand what the learning experience means to them. They look at the different associations they have with the beginning of the course. Perhaps it reminds them of their first day at school, arousing painful memories of leaving home and fears about whether they will be able to learn. Becoming aware of these connections enables members to acknowledge what it is like to start a course and to focus their energy on the other parts of the course.

CASE EXAMPLE

In a group for elderly patients and their carers in a geriatric hospital, Terry (1997) describes how the interaction in the group haltingly and painfully reflects themes of the experience of the elderly, making the group aware of the contrast between the younger sexually active staff and the impotent aged patients. Thinking about death was constantly being denied, sabotaged or avoided and Terry shows how through the interaction of the group the theme of death is faced when one of the patients sings 'Danny Boy' with such feeling that many group members, patients and staff, were in tears.

LEARNING POINTS

- The value of homogeneous groups is apparent at a common-sense level.
- Beyond the common-sense level the group-analytic approach to group structure and process can be applied to homogeneous groups to enable them to appreciate:
  1. the shared metaphors which they are using to express their underlying distress
  2. the unconscious conflicts they are struggling with which can cause difficult dynamics within the group.
- Where a homogeneous group is formed around a shared problem the life of the group may need to be limited so that members do not get stuck in their identity as a person with a particular problem. A homogeneous group can be a preparation for joining a heterogeneous group for those who need further treatment.
- Homogeneous groups can have a special value in allowing socially repressed aspects of experience to surface which might get lost in a heterogeneous group.

Conclusions

We hope that this chapter has encouraged you to include gender, race, age, historical experience and other social issues in your thinking about what is influencing the unconscious processes in the group. We have tried to show that this dimension is as much part of the group as other categories which are a more accepted aspect of the language of counselling and psychotherapy. This is a way of interpreting what Foulkes meant when he wrote about every individual being deeply imbued with the social, and suggested that every group reflects the social context within which it takes place. At times the group conductor may need to indicate that the group is repressing the social dimension just as she might suggest that anger, intimacy or competition were being avoided. This chapter argues for the importance of the conductor's own awareness of these topics being developed so that she can help them to emerge in the group.

We have also tried to show the value of offering homogeneous groups in specific situations. Research on this topic suggests that, on the whole, heterogeneous groups work at a deeper level than homogeneous ones. However, we have shown how valuable particular homogeneous groups can be. In this we have shown that the support gained by the group members' shared experience is amplified and clarified by the analytic group space which allows both the metaphorical and the unconscious aspects of members' experience to be understood. Shared unconscious themes, such as the elderly's preoccupation with death, are more likely to be brought into the foreground in the homogeneous group. This is particularly likely to be true where the subject is socially repressed, as death is, and the hothouse of the homogeneous group brings it into the open.

WORKING TOGETHER

Applying an understanding of groups in the workplace

Introduction

When students on the Groupwork course were asked about their own experiences in groups many spoke about multidisciplinary teams and staff meetings. Applying group-analytic thought and practice within the workplace requires an awareness of fundamental differences between a group designed for therapeutic purposes and one whose primary task is work orientated. While both are subject to similar unconscious processes and use similar defence mechanisms, the *purpose* of the working group is not therapy, it is work. We want to know why people at work get damaged and jobs are left undone. Emphasising the working group's **task** and its organisational **context** addresses some of the potential confusion inherent in applying unmodified therapeutic theory and practice to the world of work.

The psychoanalytic and systemic approach to understanding work in terms of role, system and task boundaries, which are violated to defend against anxiety, provides a way of thinking about the workplace which also illuminates some processes within therapy groups; similarly some insights from group-analytic theory and practice may be applicable to working groups. We have included exercises in this chapter to encourage the reader to translate from one approach to the other. However, when an outsider, with particular knowledge of group processes, is invited to help with a staff team's difficulties, she takes up the role of **consultant** (see later), rather than that of group therapist. Paradoxically, the recognition that teams and meetings are not therapy groups facilitates the application of group-analytic ideas to thinking about the workplace.

Working Together

A good starting point in thinking psychologically about organisations is *Images of Organisation* by Gareth Morgan (1986) who argues that our diverse theories about organisations are based on metaphors which lead us to understand organisations in partial ways. While seeing an organisation as a machine underpins the development of a bureaucratic organisation, other metaphors may be of the organisation as an organism, as a brain or as a culture.

Each picture tells a partial story. A bureaucratic organisation *is* like a machine, but is also a cultural phenomenon, a political one and *an expression of unconscious concerns as well*. If we only view it as a machine, we overlook the human aspects of organisation and the fact that the tasks facing organisations are much too complex and uncertain to be undertaken by machines. The machine metaphor, like others including the psychoanalytic ones, has advantages and disadvantages. As Okun (1997) wrote about the different theories of psychotherapy, the danger 'lies more in the theorist's "potential for self-delusion" that the bias does not exist than in the bias itself'.

Morgan's psychoanalytic metaphor is the image of the organisation as a psychic prison. He uses Plato's allegory of the cave with its mouth open towards a blazing fire outside. Inside the cave are people chained facing the wall of the cave with their backs to the outside world. They cannot move. All they can see are shadows of people and objects in the cave thrown onto the wall by the light of the fire behind them. Their own shadows are their only reality; they name and talk about them and have no knowledge of anything else. In the story someone escapes from the cave (the world of appearances), and his journey represents the ascent to knowledge, or insight. He discovered that their reality was just a shadowy form of a much more complex one. The cave dwellers did not accept this new interpretation, but tightened their grip on their familiar way of seeing, preferring to stay in the dark. This image shows how, in an organisation, people can create imperfect realities out of their own preoccupations, and then become trapped by them. We apply this metaphor to some examples from the health service which could also be applied to the reader's own organisation.

Psychoanalytic Ideas about Organisations and some Parallels with Group Processes

Some of the most powerful critiques of the world of appearances have come from people within the psychoanalytic tradition and we will introduce the ideas of three of them – Elliot Jacques, Wilfred Bion and Isabel Menzies-Lyth. These ideas may also be applied to group situations in earlier chapters.

Elliott Jacques and socially constructed defence mechanisms

Elliot Jacques (1953) described shared ways of managing anxiety which can bind people together within an organisation as **socially constructed defence mechanisms**. Individuals using the same external object for their projections create, between them, an unconscious level of relationship which makes policy change on the conscious level an ineffective way of intervening in an organisation.

In the following example, staff in a special hospital are anxious about treating patients who are both sick (in need of care) and dangerous (in need of control), so they are split into two subgroups, each projecting one aspect of their emotional conflict into the other, as we have seen in other groups. Nurses do not recognise the patients' need for care while psychologists avoid their desire to control the more frightening patients. The staff might appear to want to change but they have an unconscious investment in maintaining this emotional split.

CASE EXAMPLE

> A clinical psychology trainee is on a placement in a special hospital similar to one where he had worked previously as a nurse. He had been aware of a fundamental tension of values in special hospitals: is the purpose of working with patients care or control? They are hospitals but staffed, largely, by nurses. The patients have to be kept away from society but also helped.

If the organisation is to fulfil both aims, its workers need to identify both with the concerns of the social order and the disorderly individual (see Woodhouse and Pengelly, 1991).

> He was uncomfortable both with his new colleagues' hostility towards the nurses' preoccupation with control, and with his memories of how hostile his nursing colleagues were toward psychologists, psychotherapists and psychiatrists. It did not surprise him that a characteristic defence against

the anxiety generated by deviant behaviour is to hold fast to structure. He knew how alarming a minority of the patients could be (those who had committed awful sexual or violent offences) for a nurse or a psychologist to work with, partly because the workers may be aware of similar hidden impulses in themselves.

He remembered a psychotherapist from his nursing days in a special hospital saying that the staff member was unlikely to have committed a dreadful crime, or even thought about doing so, but that they probably had dreamed about doing it.

Nurses and psychologists feel very anxious when they try to grapple with society's demand that they see their charges as both patients, 'in need of care', and criminals, 'in need of control'. The anxiety may push them away from facing the conflicting demands (Woodhouse and Pengelly, 1991), and instead they split them up along professional lines, workers hold onto only one and lose the other. Care and control are split. Psychologists and nurses are split. By analogy, mother and father are split too. The psychologist–carers then project their own impulses to control into the nurse–Prison Officers' Association and denigrate them as brutal. Projection in the other direction portrays the psychologist–carers as ineffectual and indulgent. Each group could denigrate the other and neither had to grapple with how to bring the two aspects of their task together.

The trainee clinical psychologist saw that his new colleagues were unaware of their own hostility and prejudice, not noticing those nurses who were trying to work therapeutically.

As Jacques said, the carers were bound together in a shared way of managing anxiety. The psychologists and the nursing staff were using each other to contain their projections.

The ex-nurse was aware both that the psychological metaphor has its limitations and of the brutal treatment of some of the patients.

Jacques' analysis told him how the organisation's task had been split, with the two sides becoming caricatures of themselves, leading to a deadlock. He saw a parallel with the family – mother and father in conflict and the children whose development was impaired – and knew that things had to change for the patients' sake. He recognised that recent enquiries into bad practice would only lead to better practice if the deeper anxieties of the task were recognised. Otherwise they would be voiced in another conflict, no matter how rational policy changes appeared to be.

LEARNING POINTS

■ Splitting and projecting as a way of dealing with anxiety happens both in individuals and within a group. In this book we have emphasised the importance of subgrouping where the splits can be used by the group conductor and the group to explore and resolve an underlying conflict.

> **EXERCISE** Look at Chapter 4 and see if you can identify when, why and how this happens.

Wilfred Bion: work groups and basic assumption groups

Wilfred Bion (1961) described some of the unconscious processes which are always bubbling under the surface of every **work group** making it difficult to relate realistically in a shared task. By work group Bion meant a group which is addressing its aims through working together with its task in mind. People contribute actively, allowing anyone with particular competence appropriate space, without relieving others of responsibility. The group is open to differences and new ideas, conflict is examined, roles are distinguished from people so that comments are not meant or taken personally, there is a spirit of co-operation but members are not afraid of losing their individuality. This state of affairs rarely lasts very long in any meeting before we are stuck, or angry, or joking, or bored, or bickering. Bion's comment on these derailments was that: 'A certain cohesion is given to these anomalous mental activities if it is assumed that emotionally the group acts *as if* it had certain basic assumptions about its aims' (1961, our italics).

He formulated these basic assumptions as **dependence, pairing** and **fight or flight** and speaks of a group dominated by one of them as a **basic assumption group**. These are not physical groups but metaphors. That is, when the job of a team or group provokes anxiety it may act, for defensive purposes, *as if* the members were sharing a common basic assumption – *as if* they were there for something else. Unconsciously, the members feel their survival is threatened and fantasise that their move into basic assumption mode will protect them. There are deep underlying anxieties hidden away in many institutions and organisations, as in the example of the special hospital. Our actual visible work groups flip in and out of basic assumption modality.

In a group that has flipped into the dependence basic assumption – the unofficial aim is to obtain security from a powerful leader who might either be the person with authority or a substitute, for example the former boss or a book of rules. The group denies any need for competence, creativity or individual differences, projecting omnipotence onto this *leader.* The reader may have had the experience of conducting a group, or chairing a meeting, or leading a seminar when everyone looks abandoned and confused and you get the horrible feeling that they are expecting you to deal with the situation even though you know they could do it themselves. Such countertransference in a work group setting is as fruitful a source of understanding as it is in group therapy.

In the pairing group the shared unconscious assumption is that the group, instead of facing and overcoming difficulties through collaborative effort, will produce an ideal pair who will give birth to a *messiah* (a group saviour). The atmosphere is often optimistic and flirtatious. Hope for the future is used as a defence against the difficulties of the task in the present.

> At a meeting which does not address the implications of making a choice, three members were asked to integrate the two proposals. At the next meeting nobody mentioned the item.

The members cannot face the fact that they will have to make a choice so they procrastinate and appear to forget the issue. Current difficulties are shelved in the hope that they will go away until the spring, the 'away day' or the next election. Similarly, in the experiential group in Chapter 4, the members cannot face group anxieties and focus on a potential romance outside the group.

In the fight or flight group members seem to be there to fight with or flee from somebody or something rather than to work together effectively. The group behaves as if it were under attack, or about to be, and paranoid myths and fantasies abound.

When this basic assumption prevails a state of lawlessness leads to the survival of the fittest.

> A hospital is preparing to become a Trust and the recently appointed directors are meeting for the first time, after months of rumours. They are all new to management and to each other. All they are sure of is that money is scarce and will get scarcer. The entire meeting is spent vilifying a particular occupational group, a low status one not on the committee, which was 'overstaffed', 'overfunded' and 'never did anything'. One of the directors was silent, feeling uncomfortable but not knowing the group under discussion. Afterwards she discovered that the group were well thought of.

It was as if the meeting were there to destroy something, instead of facing its own difficult and frightening tasks, and to her shame she had felt unable to intervene.

Bion saw the basic assumptions as an instinctual response to the experience of being in a group. Their hidden agenda is the continuance or survival of the group rather than the difficult job the individuals somehow have to find a way of tackling together. They appear to be easier options than working for change and haunt every group and organisation. Bion suggested that any group oscillates between *basic assumptions* and actual *work;* between external reality and internal unreality. The question is how we limit or use this propensity for the benefit of the task. It is the ratio between the two that determines the ultimate effectiveness of the group.

LEARNING POINTS

■ Bion's ideas illuminate the working group with its set (pursued/avoided) task. They also apply to the therapy group which can act as if its purpose is dependence, pairing or flight or fight rather than therapy. The 'group as a whole' is working against 'therapy in the group, of the group, and by the group'. Identifying a basic assumption mode is helpful to the consultants and conductors.

EXERCISE   Can any of the clinical examples in this book be usefully seen in this light?

Isabel Menzies-Lyth: an illustration of social defences within the nursing profession

Isabel Menzies-Lyth's (1959) study of the nurses in a British hospital is an excellent example of the cave dwellers' world. She observed that the nurses' (cave dwellers') practices at work seemed designed to help nurses to contain *their* anxieties about working with sick and dying people, by depersonalising their relationships with them, rather than for the patients' benefit. A patient could just be 'the liver in bed ten', while nurses' uniforms made them part of a faceless army of interchangeable helpers. Such rituals, which Jacques (1955) termed **social defences**, help people not to think, and not thinking helps people not to feel anxious.

Menzies-Lyth recognised that, as in the example in the special hospital setting, nursing exposes people in real life to situations and feelings that trouble the rest of us in our dreams. The mix up between fantasy and reality creates anxiety; nurses know what their roles and tasks are in relation to their patients, but also unconsciously (as in a dream) are aware of the other associations they may have to performing these tasks. She concluded that the *objective situation confronting the nurse,* the actual job, bears a striking relationship to infantile fantasy situations as described by Melanie Klein. The nurses used the rituals' new authority to justify their depersonalised relationships. Individual nurses collude in operating the same defences and shape the culture of an institution. These *social defences* are *institutionalised* and become external realities independent of the individuals involved. Like the shadows in the cave they are taken for reality. The defences become part of the institution and affect the personalities of the people involved. Social defences solve nothing; they allow the institution to short circuit anxiety and prevent it from learning. There is no space for thinking – no space where feelings may be discussed.

Although nowadays there is a new emphasis on the continuity of nurse–patient relationships, how this is influencing the social defences of nursing remains to be seen. Where the demand is for evidence-based clinical practice, time for discussion and supervision can be seen as a luxury no one can afford. The psychoanalytic approach challenges the prevailing overrational view of organisations. Our so-called efficient procedures may be irrationality in disguise; memoranda and faxed papers can contain the anxiety of face-to-face communication.

Hirschorn (1998) added another layer of social defences, termed **covert coalitions**, where anxiety is evaded by engaging in family alliances, rather than working in collaboration on the difficult task in hand.

When defence mechanisms such as splitting and projection, reverting to basic assumption groups or to old family scripts are used in a therapy group, members and the group conductor pursue their task of understanding the group processes and enhancing the group communication, which benefits the individual group members. In the work setting the task is different and a way has to be found to make use of these insights into the *cave.*

EXERCISE Find some illustrations of this process in the examples in the book. Can you think of examples from your workplace?

- The purposes of therapy groups and working groups are different.
- Working within the organisational setting has led to the use of further concepts about group processes, some of which can also be applied to therapy groups.
- In a therapy group a group member unconsciously tries to fit the other group members into a family script. Often the group conductor will be cast as a parent. This can be used defensively to avoid taking up relevant issues but also allows an old stuck relationship to be worked on within the new setting of the group.

Applying Group-analytic Thinking to the Workplace: The Role of Consultation

Most readers of this book will want to apply the ideas outlined so far to understanding their own staff teams or obtaining help to do so. Others may be asked as a group therapist to *do* a staff group. Here we describe how these ideas can be applied to an organisation through the role of the consultant and its relationship to the role of group therapist. Neither group therapist nor consultant takes a request for a particular sort of help at face value. Just as the group therapist thinks about the appropriateness of setting up a particular sort of group in a given context and in assessing potential group members' suitability for therapy in a group, so the request for help in the workplace requires forethought too. It is well worth spending time on clarifying a request, for instance for a staff group, and trying to understand with the client what it is a request *for*. The consultant does not enter the workplace with a specific expertise to offer but assists the client in this process of clarification (Schein, 1987).

An organisation asks for *help* when it is stuck, and hanging onto unproductive behaviour which avoids mental pain. The request may be an ambivalent one: something like 'cure us but don't change us'.

Before she leaves her preliminary meeting with a manager a consultant asks if there is a better parking place than the distant multistorey she'd had to use. He takes her to the window and points down to the busy street below saying, 'You can park down there on the double yellow lines. The traffic wardens don't come round that often.' As she walks out of the building, passing a traffic warden, she reflected on what seemed a highly promising meeting with an insightful and highly motivated manager. Nonetheless, she did not feel welcome.

A request for a staff group is not simply the offer of an already established group for a conductor to work with, but may be the only way of expressing an answer to a question which has not yet been formulated, perhaps because it is too dangerous. The prospective consultant must attend to the processes leading up to the request, to ensure that she has not been asked in to preside over the release of the mob: spleen may be vented, blood spilt, tears shed, things said and damage done – *and it will all be her fault!* She can carry away all the blame. Or she may be asked in by the staff to undermine the manager or by the manager to sort out the staff. Or she may find that the group whose communication she is supposed to help improve never meets. They need to consider how to meet first. Sometimes a staff group may be what is required and the initial thorough discussion provides a solid starting point.

LEARNING POINTS

- When individuals or groups have difficulties in an organisational context they need someone to engage with in the role of consultant rather than therapist.
- The process consultant is there to help the consultee/client define the problem before any remedy is offered.
- The request for a consultation will itself be subject to scrutiny since it may well be the outcome of the consultee's ambivalence about change.
- The initial work of the consultant can be compared to the group conductor's dynamic administration.
- In therapy groups and in consulting to organisations an awareness of the significance of maintaining and breaking boundaries is maintained.

Similarities and Differences between Consultation and Group Therapy

Consultation is about *work*. It aims to help people to be more effective at work through an awareness and understanding of psychological processes. The purpose of the therapy group is therapy, and the conductor sets a clear boundary between it and the surrounding organisation so that therapy can take place (see Chapters 3 and 5). The consultee group is not a patient group in need of the therapist's expertise, but is a competent group of workers who are consulting us as professional equals on a matter within the domain of *their* expertise. Therapists look at *personal relationships*, but consultants are concerned with **relatedness**. People at work have a relatedness to each other whether they like it or not, and whether they like each other or not. They are related by their **roles** in a system they have in common, which is working towards a common task.

As persons taking up roles and facing the reality of work they are relating to each other as whole objects. However, as Hirschorn has shown (1998), the task may arouse such anxiety that people retreat from their official roles and violate one another. The consultant seeks to understand how *unofficial* vacancies arise on the unconscious notice board; how is one person (or a subgroup) used to express something on behalf of the whole group? Is the person who is seen as incompetent and inept unconsciously asked to carry this projection for everyone else? Projective identification is the key to shifting from an individual perspective (of dysfunctional person) or an interpersonal one (of personality clashes) to a group-as-a-whole perspective (what is being expressed on behalf of the group?). The consultant is a likely target for such projections. The group-analytic psychotherapist is familiar with these three levels. In her work with staff groups and teams, she emphasises the third perspective and its relationship to the task of the working group. The group-analytic approach offers a rich understanding of working life once these adjustments of perspective are made.

The primary task

CASE EXAMPLE

> A consultant met with a team of therapists and counsellors for a few initial sessions. Her first impression was of a welcoming and eager group. She was oddly uncomfortable about being called by her first name and felt she was being stuffy. They seemed to find her persistent question about what they hoped to gain from her intervention a nuisance. They made some personal disclosures to illustrate their desire for more 'openness'. These, she felt, were news only to her. Neither could she discover the **primary task** of the service.

The primary task is what a group or organisation is there *for,* like Bion's work group. The basic assumptions are what the group looks *as if* it is there for. The consultant thinks about whether the group's practices engage with the environment in a way which serves its stated task – or whether they express the group's need to avoid the outside world and engage in **anti-task** wish fulfilment?

The group offered their mission statement: to provide a high-class service to all the deprived people in a poor city. This was to be achieved on a shoestring by staff with either a minimal training or an individual long-term therapy training. Was this omnipotent? Were they worried about what their real impact might be?

Meetings started late as they waited for everyone. Long-suffering looks were exchanged when she queried this, as if to say 'here she goes again'. The consultant was subtly put in the dilemma of joining them in their boundaryless mellow blur or being a strident fusspot.

She forgot their names. It was as if, she reflected, they did not quite exist as separate individuals, as if the only difference in the room was when she tried to stay on task as a consultant; she was the outcast. Yet she knew that some had had more training than others; that they belonged to different professions; that there had to be some role related-ness and authority issues around line management, in the blur created by the staff. There was also the unmentionable fact that some must be paid more and some less for doing the same job. She was aware that she was taking on many of the feelings that belonged in the group – being not up to the job, uncared for, confused and angry as well as having an unnat-ural interest in status, power, authority and money, as if such things were not spoken about in polite caring professional society. To act as a consultant in this group would be outrageously individualistic, a social gaffe for which she would be cast out.

The **pseudomutual group** (Gustafson, 1976) is disarmingly open and unselfish but blurs all distinctions and boundaries; a more subtle version of Bion's (1961) basic assumption groups. Language is muddled and words sound right but are imprecise. All differences including pay and power differentials are flattened and the boundaries of disagreement are obscured. The sources of divergence between leadership and followership and even the boundaries of the self and those between the group and the outside world are smudged. Bion (1961), like Foulkes (1948), taught us that we are social animals and that we cannot get on without each other but he unfortunately said that we also cannot get on *with* each other either. The tension between the individual and the group was acted out with the consultant representing the outsider, the 'singleton' (see Turquet, 1975), who can be controlled from their snug nest. The consultant's task in such groups is to clarify the critical boundaries that are being actively obscured.

Countertransference

The consultant felt controlled by the group – but the group did not have control of her mind for she was able to think about the processes that occur in the group's environment as *experienced first hand by herself;* that is, countertransference. As in therapy, there is always the danger that the *counter* in countertransference is either the counterpart of trans-ference or something happening to counteract it. But we know from psychotherapy that in spite of the dangers, it is worth taking our emotional responses seriously.

Probably the first reference to countertransference in groups is early in Bion's *Experiences in Groups* (1961) where he writes: 'Furthermore, I am aware of feeling uneasily that I am expected to do something.' It is upon this feeling that he developed his basic assumption theory, which shows us that the leader is only allowed to lead when she fits the basic assumption in question. The consultant is expected to be the *right sort* of leader too, and when she tries to be a consultant instead she is quickly deposed. What Bion discovered was that her feelings can tell her which kind of basic assumption leader she is supposed to be. In the covert coalition, the consultant feels drawn into enacting a family script. The consultant's feeling response to **organisational rituals** will be to the sheer impact of its culture, which someone who has worked there for years will be unaware of.

Whatever the social defence, the consultant feels it: the denied anger or sadness or confusion. Her experiences in the context of the organisation are a response to its unconscious processes. She may be able to put words to the unnameable missing aspects of the organisa-tion's attempts to work together. She may feel what is missing by empathic identification or by identification with what is projected. We know from working as therapists, and from our experiences in groups, that someone evoking their feelings in others is a way of communi-cating their troubling experience. The unacceptable is projected into the other but held onto because of ambivalence toward it, it is still there – now in a more controllable way – and with the wish that someone may do something about it (without any sense of what *it* or the *something* may be). This is a defence against what is hard to bear. The consultant can use her feelings to understand the staff's experi-ences and to help the staff to understand them too. After all it is easier for the consultant. As one staff member said to their consultant: *'You're* confused! You're only here an hour a week, we're here day in day out – you can see what it is like.'

Containment

The confusion described in the earlier section is a signal that the staff need help in re-owning their feelings and projections, which have emerged in the consultant's countertransference. The consultant provides an appropriate environment for them to surface and be presented back to a staff group, which is ready to think about them, in a manageable form.

> In a community mental health agency caring for chronic patients, what was difficult to accept was their hatred of the clients for being so demanding, ungrateful and unrewarding. Instead, a more congenial image of carers was preserved by blaming managers who don't care and just tread all over people, clients and staff, for the limitations of the service and its apparent ineffectiveness.

Hating the patient or client can always be projected elsewhere. Someone else can be criticised as self-interested and anti-therapeutic; another team or the *management*. Organisations have to have their component parts and must be managed, so necessary structural divisions between sub-systems of the organisation can offer up the arenas for playing out projections of negative and split-off images of the work, especially where there are no opportunities for testing the reality of the projections. Such opportunities are avoided anyway, as they challenge the defence. If, however, less acceptable aspects are acknowledged as projections and withdrawn, the consultees must recognise that they have misused someone and face the discomfort of the unwanted thought or feeling being their own. This eventually happened in the staff group at the community mental health agency.

A large part of the consultant's work is containing what is first split and then projected. She helps the group to move from paranoid-schizoid functioning to the depressive position. No one individual is left to *carry the can* full of the split-off aspects of the group; nor do subgroups serve as conduits for the conflicting wishes and fears involved in doing a job that evokes much the *same* wishes and fears in most of the people trying to do it. But we must note Bion's two-way arrow between the two 'positions' – we can move between the two; splitting and projection beckon in even the most sophisticated of teams when there seems to be too much reality to bear.

Thinking in this way can help any member of a staff team to understand some of the underlying processes in the workplace, or in team or interteam meetings. It also clarifies what a consultant's intervention or setting up of a staff group can offer.

LEARNING POINTS

- A consultant working in a staff group uses group-analytic skills, drawing out group processes, particularly focusing on the subgroup and whole group levels.
- A group in need of a consultant often has to have its projected split-off parts contained so that it can move from the paranoid-schizoid towards the depressive position.
- Like the group therapist, the consultant's countertransference is one of her main tools for understanding the group and particularly identifying what is unacceptable to the group.

Thinking about the Whole Organisation

Individualising group phenomena

Institutional difficulties or chaos are often personalised, being seen as caused by a neurotic individual, personality clashes or the difficulties of a particular team needing therapeutic intervention. People need help in finding their roles within the structures relating to their tasks before any therapeutic intervention is considered.

The work of the various helping professions, which we will focus on here, is *intrinsically* anxiety making, as Menzies-Lyth (1959) showed. Indeed, the whole National Health Service could be seen as a giant unconscious container for the anxieties arising from our awareness of illness, our mortality and inevitable death (Obholzer, 1994), leaving all its workers vulnerable to swallowing projections of societal fantasies concerning their omnipotence. But their daily experience is rarely of dramatic cure or life-giving rescue, rather a matter of trying to take decent care of people in physical or mental pain.

The gap undermines the workers' sense of competence. Unfortunately, both their training and management rhetoric may have emphasised competence at the expense of recognising the emotional reality of task-related anxiety (see Mollon, 1989, for an examination of clinical psychology training). From training to retirement, there is rarely any officially sanctioned opportunity to talk about what it is *like* to be in the helping professions. Woodhouse and Pengelly (1991) identified characteristic anxieties associated with, and specific to, each of five professions. When these competent professionals were given the space to think and talk about their work it was possible to identify the *task-*

related anxieties they had in common with their colleagues, rather than individual neurotic problems. They relied less on their professionally acquired defences and could discuss their human experience and fallibility. This meant that they were more likely to think about their difficulties rather than projecting their anxieties or acting them out. Opportunities for such work discussion make people more competent.

Intergroup processes

The main concern of Woodhouse and Pengelly was the dynamics of the collaboration *between* professions and they observed that when a case was difficult and disturbing, each profession retreated behind its own particular unconscious social defence. Thus the different professions do not co-operate very well on an interagency or interdisciplinary basis when the emotional stakes are high. It is like Foulkes' description of people in a therapy group: members of different professions become pieces from different jigsaw puzzles – they do not fit. We are all familiar with what happens next: crossed wires, rivalry, righteous indignation, sabotage, secrecy, flattery, umbrage, vague threats, blame, fear and loathing. These are signs that defences have been mobilised, and the underlying anxieties need to be identified before any real shared work can be done.

Yet when each person has a clearly demarcated role, with a clear authority structure and team task, they can work interdependently and with good management can be brought back on task together. However in the health service things are changing and the new multidisciplinary team culture seeks the right 'skills mix', blurring old boundaries. When professional identities and securities are threatened, inarticulate *primitive anxiety* is mobilised. Zealously pursued change can appear to undervalue previously gained experience. With no clarity about new roles and overall strategy, staff feel confused, anxious or incompetent. Difficult or unwanted aspects of ourselves that were previously managed by upward or sideways projection into established *others* are leeched down to the interpersonal arena of individual members within an organisation leading to personality clashes, gossip, stress in workers and middle managers, bullying and scapegoating. Institutional chaos is personalised, as it is in the multidisciplinary team.

Skynner (1989) describes how task-related anxieties can be worked with productively at different levels according to the group's readiness for personal exploration. However, any approach to the intrinsic anxieties of a particular job done by a group of people will be undermined if the *extrinsic* anxieties of unclear roles, systems and tasks have pushed them so far along the 'anxiety curve' that functioning is a struggle. Extrinsic anxiety must be reduced before intrinsic anxiety can be contained.

LEARNING POINTS

- When an awkward individual *appears* to be the cause of the problem, this is understood in terms of the person's role within the staff team rather than a need for personal counselling.
- In multidisciplinary work each profession has its own defence structure which can interfere with co-operative work. A containing setting enables professionals to acknowledge their fallibility.

Conclusion: Group Analysis and Group Relations

Many group-analytic skills and ideas are applicable to organisations as long as we remember that we are trying to understand people in their work roles and how they might feel and act more effectively at work. The group-analytic use of interpretations and emphasis on boundaries can be applied to organisations. The concepts of splitting and projection and group-specific phenomena remain fruitful. While all therapists know how to listen to their feelings, group-analytic training hones the capacity to listen within the particular pressures of a group setting. If we listen to the voice of our own feelings we can encourage other staff members (including managers) to stand back from appearances and the sheer impact of their reality to use *their* own feelings to understand what is going on; and where this is no longer possible to use a consultant to facilitate such thinking.

Thinking space is decreasing, particularly in education and the health and social services. Learning about group therapy provides insights into the psychology of groups applicable to the work setting. A nurse manager will not make interpretations to her ward staff, but she may use her authority differently. Everyone who has responsibility for others at work can reduce extrinsic anxiety by taking up clear roles in relation to manageable tasks, encouraging others to do likewise, and using the structures of authority and collaboration available to support this intention. We can make supervision and opportunities for case discussion and appropriate training our priorities with regard to those intrinsic anxieties of the work often overlooked by senior managers. By creating spaces for thinking which privilege feelings, people see how they collude with what afflicts them, distinguish imaginary persecutors from real enemies and return to work. They may even use their authority to change work for the better.

9

ON BECOMING A
GROUP THERAPIST

Introduction

What qualities does a group conductor need? What does this imply for a model of further development for those who want to continue their work in groups without becoming professionally qualified as a group analyst? The new group therapist is subject to particular pressures and must consider her personal and professional needs carefully. This book has shown how the personal characteristics of the group therapist form the basis for her capacity to work in groups. Monitoring and analysing her countertransference, will enable her to stay *in role* in the group. We outline some of the tools and contexts which facilitate professional development and give practical details about obtaining information on group training from an analytic perspective.

Personal and professional development are an ongoing process, guided by the individual's goals, structured by ethical standards, and influenced by increasing self-knowledge from clinical experience, theory and research. Abuse occurs down the blind alleys, the dead ends of development.

The Orientation of the New Group Therapist

The experience of starting out

The situations faced by the new group therapist seem to have broad similarities across many different institutions. Some may offer little opportunity to use the skills which have been learned while others appear to be supportive but subtly sabotage new group initiatives. A nurse may decide, on the basis of her introductory training, to set up an exploratory analytic group and no one seems to mind: except that her group room keeps being double-booked, or a doctor unexpectedly turns up in a session to *observe* and give occasional instruction, or she finds she has to cover someone off sick on the ward when she should be conducting her group, or a member announces that he has been told to leave the group by the person who referred him to it because it is not doing him any good.

While one person may feel persecuted by trying to run a group, someone else may feel equally persecuted *into* running one, having been sent to *do a group* on a difficult ward or having been ordered to take over an existing group because its leader has left, in both cases starting next week. Beginning therapists have found themselves *volunteered* to *do groups* alone or with others without any room for manoeuvre or any space for thinking about setting up the group experience. However great the pressure, there is too much at stake in complying – the therapeutic potential of the group for its members, the reputation of group therapy and the new conductor's development and confidence.

Yet another course member may get the opportunity to co-conduct a group with a senior colleague who has had considerable training and experience. Meanwhile, her peer on the course, equally keen to get started with groups, finds herself co-conducting a group with a colleague who, while certainly senior to the point of being her line manager, knows a lot less about groups than she does but will not admit it. One person may be frustrated at only being allowed to run brief focal structured groups by her boss while another is content to apply what she has learned from the less structured ways of group analysis to her anxiety management groups.

The places where many beginners work are not always supportive of group psychotherapy, or further training. We are aware that, while groups have enormous therapeutic potential, they also evoke powerful and hidden feelings, both in those who are inside them and those who are not. It may be that this partly explains why group therapy in particular evokes such a strong institutional response; although we must acknowledge that counselling and analytic psychotherapy can also meet with this kind of subtle institutional discouragement and sabotage. Yet although becoming a group therapist can be quite a struggle most of those who begin seem determined to continue.

The question is: what needs to happen to facilitate becoming a group therapist?

As they leave the final session of the introductory course different people take different paths across different terrains with different aims in mind. People may stop somewhere along them and consider other paths in the light of their experience. The next few years could be a developmental moratorium in which things are mulled over awaiting the right internal and external conditions for going any further with group therapy. Or a lot may happen. For instance someone may start out simply with a new interest in how her multidisciplinary team works and with fresh insights into the social skills training groups she runs. Then she may set up an exploratory therapy group, and then another and eventually find herself spending a lot of the working week conducting groups of one sort or another and considering a specialist training.

Personal characteristics of the group therapist

Along the many developmental paths towards becoming a group therapist certain ingredients are vital. First, she must be open to continuous development and change. Foulkes said: 'Prepare yourself well. Your knowledge is never finally achieved. You are continuously working at yourself in your activity and function. *Your conducting is a continuous learning, but this should not be at the expense of the group'* (1975, italics added).

Second, she needs to be spontaneous, responsive and direct (Grotjahn, 1983). She must trust herself and have confidence in the group. Her personal identity should be clear so that she is recognised (and recognises herself) for the person that she is. She must be aware of the complexity of relationships that develop in a group, the transferences to her, to the group members and to the group as a whole. This, in turn, will enable her to use her countertransference for the benefit of the group.

Developmental phases

An introductory course lays down the foundations for establishing a group and taking up the role of group therapist. It has been said of many a job that you can learn half of it relatively quickly but that the other half takes a lifetime. Skovholt and Ronnestad (1992), in their study of therapist and counsellor development, looked at what happened in the often long professional lives of their subjects. They analysed hundreds of interviews with students and professional workers in the fields of, mainly, clinical and counselling psychology and proposed an eight-stage model of therapist/counsellor development running from no training at all (conventional stage) to preparing for retirement (integrity stage). If all goes well they noted a growth in relying on oneself rather than external experts.

Skovholt and Ronnestad illustrate how new challenges and complexities arise with *each stage* and argue that the prerequisite for development is the ability to stay open to, and to reflect upon, the diversity and complexity of phenomena and processes that unfold throughout a career. Stagnation occurs in the absence of such continuous reflection and leads either to leaving one's job or to fending off its intrinsic anxieties by premature closure. The latter route leads to what they call pseudo-development – apparent development disguising defensive and repetitive professional functioning. In the earlier developmental stages, therapists want things to be cut and dried; they may want, to use a phrase of Bowlby's (1979), to pour a quart of obstreperous human nature into a pint pot of prim theory. The anxious awareness that this will not work and that things are more complicated than were first thought can lead to exploratory reflection or defensive closure.

Here we are principally concerned with how to maintain development after the introductory course. At this stage, according to Skovholt and Ronnestad, trainees will have assimilated information from many sources and will be trying to apply it in practice, notably by imitating experts as a way station to conditional autonomy as therapists themselves. Affectively, this will initially involve enthusiasm and insecurity followed by bewildering ups and downs before a degree of confidence begins to set in.

However, the disillusionment of the newish group therapist, as with the distress of the seasoned practitioner and the regret of one nearing retirement, can prompt further exploration and development. Tolerating disillusionment is an achievement in itself. The group poses dangers for the therapist who hangs on to her illusions. There may be a lot of personal and professional esteem riding on the group for the therapist. It may have to live up to expectations from the good groups in the books studied and perhaps to the way that the introductory course experiential group leader seemed to know what she was doing. The therapist may have had to argue the therapeutic potential of groups and her own competency in conducting them in the face of opposition to the point that she has set herself standards that anyone would have difficulty in meeting. New information needs to enter such a system. In the next section we present some of these ways in which we can learn from opening up our practice to minds other than our own.

Tools for Development

Group therapists can seek further development through:

- observing a group
- being a co-therapist
- studying theory
- becoming a member of a group
- supervision.

Foulkes, as we know, developed a 'psychotherapy by the group, of the group, including the conductor' where the therapist is *in* the group, rather than in a dyadic relationship to it, and *learning*. Those who want to continue their development as group therapists will find their practice and further learning is often opened up using these developmental tools. Some will want to continue in professional group-analytic training, which holds firm a space for thinking that can be internalised and carried forward after qualification into the lifetime's work of further learning.

Observing groups

Foulkes (1975) commented on the value of *auxiliary* methods of learning whereby trainees get the opportunity to see, in one way or another, what is actually going on in groups conducted by more experienced therapists. Beginning therapists often express a desire for such opportunities. Wanting to see an *expert* at work, avoiding complex theories and generally moving towards tight construing in the early days of becoming a therapist can all be located developmentally.

Group therapy can be most closely observed, literally, by sitting either in or just outside the circle of a real live group. Group members should be informed of the presence and purpose of the observer in advance. The role of the silent observer must be clear to everyone. As we pointed out in Chapter 1, the observer both notices what she actually sees and hears and notes what she feels. Being incommunicado in the thick of the group experience can be disturbing.

It is impossible to observe without influencing what is being observed. Cappielo *et al.* (1988) believe that the silent observer can have a positive influence by receiving some of the negative transferences which would normally have interfered with the conductor's integration with the group. Lear (1988), asked himself: 'If the silent observer is good for the patients, is it also good for silent observer?' It is vital that the conductor, in her training role, schedules in time for a post-group discussion.

Another way of observing groups is from behind a one-way screen. This method seems less threatening for the observer and allows several people to learn from observation at the same time, discussing the group as it is going on. It is easier to ignore the background paraphernalia of microphone/camera/screen than a flesh and blood observer, and therefore it is too easy for all concerned to collude in avoiding the issues generated (Hobbs, 1988). The psychological boundaries of the group are extended into the next room where another group is sitting. Physically, however, the screen reflects back the images of the therapy group in the room providing a literal mirroring which will affect individuals differently.

Critical disapproving aspects of members are projected, as with the silent observer, but now on to faceless people. The observers are shielded by gadgetry and the group cannot look them in the eyes. The group may (apparently) agree to being observed and may not refer overtly to the arrangements thereafter. But Hobbs shows how screening a group brings new twists and turns to the group process. *If the reactions of the group are acknowledged and interpreted* it can contribute to therapy. The difficulty is that if the conductor feels judged from behind the screen she may collude with the group in ignoring its effect on resistances and fantasies. If the effect the observers are having on the observed can be addressed, the observers, too, will have a better learning experience.

Many organisations in which group therapy is practised would be willing to consider people who have had an introductory training observing groups. It is necessary to observe a group over time so that a sense of its development is acquired and understood.

Sometimes conductors videotape sessions and discuss them with trainees rather than having them behind a screen. Some therapists keep tapes of a few sessions which they use occasionally for teaching purposes to illustrate particular themes or concepts and, similarly, professionally made videotapes are available which give a sense of what it is like to conduct a group. Although no substitute for observing a group over time, viewing tapes of discreet sessions can to some extent meet the desire of seeing what expert conductors really get up to. Another valuable insight is provided by Kennard *et al.* (1993), whose workbook illustrates how different conductors say they would have intervened in a series of highly realistic events in the life of a group. Although all the conductors who contributed to this project share the same group-analytic stance it is refreshing for newer therapists to discover how differently each conductor articulates the orientation they have in common. This is a small but significant step from the natural desire to imitate experts along the developmental path to a more personal style.

Being a co-therapist

People often conduct their first group with someone else. Yalom (1995, p. 414) believes that co-conducting has special advantages for *beginning* therapists. They can learn from each other because they see different things – literally, because they are sitting in different places, but also cognitively in terms of their own views of people and emotionally because they will resonate differently to the same events in the life of the group. They feel less anxious about starting and conducting a group. Co-conductors can give each other feedback about how they are coming across in a group; information they would not have access to otherwise. If two new therapists feel they have a chance of working reasonably well together and are able to make a commitment towards open discussion in post-group sessions, preferably with joint supervision as well, this is indeed a tool for development. When one group conductor is more experienced this needs to be acknowledged. The senior partner may fear losing face while the junior one worries about being in the other's shadow. The newer person may have a freshness and capacity to empathise with group members which need adequate recognition. Once the relationship is made explicit, both can contribute their particular skills and experience to the group.

Groups have a potential for splitting co-conductors which can be turned to therapeutic advantage if they have a good enough relationship; this might be defined as having mutual respect and a capacity to discuss their experience including controversial and negative emotions. As in the Kennard *et al.* workbook just alluded to, where conductors take up their role from the same group-analytic stance but act differently, co-conductors can be clearly different persons while sharing a common perspective and set of values concerning their group. The mix of similarities and differences that is important to group composition is also invaluable in the co-conductor couple (see Whitaker, 1985). The group experiences two adults collaborating in the service of everyone in the group. This can be in stark contrast to earlier parental experiences of destructive competition, where behaviour is modified for one or the other parent, or sides have to be taken.

The family metaphor is heightened if the conductors are a man and a woman, with the added advantage of seeing a male/female couple co-operating in a less conflicted power relationship than is usual. However two same-sex conductors can be split in the transference into mother and father. It is more important for the co-conductors to be able to work together than to feel pressured to provide a symbolic male–female couple for their group.

Planning the group together allows prospective co-conductors to discover to what extent they have similar aims, objectives and theoretical perspectives and whether a sufficient sense of personal compatibility emerges. If they avoid this, what looks like simple expediency may be a conscious or unconscious reflection of their tenuous commitment to working together for the group. When such an arrangement is set up because one of the co-conductors cannot refuse, it does not auger well for the power relations between the conductors. Either way, it can lay down the fault lines along which the group may split later on.

Co-conductors make two parental transference objects available. As with the silent observer, this allows positive and negative transferences to be unravelled and laid out before the group in a less complicated way than when the one person is the object of, say, strong feelings of love *and* hate. One therapist can shed light on what the group is doing to her colleague – but, this time, the colleague is allowed to speak too. The way in which the group divides the two conductors may reflect the group's themes. In a group for women who have been sexually abused, one conductor may become the abuser while the other may be the silent unprotesting parent. The splitting of the conductors into a *good* one and a *bad* one can be therapeutic if the conductors can distinguish between fantasy and reality. If they are concerned about who is really good and bad, the split will become part of the group's *reality* and amplified accordingly in a way that will be anti-therapeutic.

Using the two conductors differently is potential grist for the therapeutic mill. When their relationship is more tentative and anxious they may not have the confidence to explore gender, experience or status differences with the group but may interpret *all* differentiations between them as transference. If the relationship is frankly bad, they will foster what is destructive in the group. Conductors cannot contain for the group what they cannot tolerate for themselves so new co-conductors should always have their supervision, their space for thinking about the group, arranged *as a pair* at the outset. If one of the crucial parts of learning as a group therapist is achieved through exploration of the countertransference, for co-therapists it may be a difficult, controversial but essential area of discussion.

Theory

Foulkes believed that the analytic attitude developed by group-analytic training could not be learned from books alone. He also wrote: 'It should however be stressed that we cannot learn it either from experience alone. Intensive study and work are necessary, reading and thinking in addition to personal experience' (1975, p. 162). The question then becomes what theoretical direction to take.

Schafer's (1983) distinction between fictions and myths is of relevance. A fiction is a structuring principal which seems significant and useful as a partial view of reality but which is not mistaken *for* reality. Therapists need to have their structuring principals, their theories, in order to construe what is happening in therapy. Frank and Frank's (1991) review of the research confirms Skovholt and Ronnestad (1992) who suggest that having a theory (and integrating it) is more important than which theory you hold. But when schools make their competing professional claims they can lose sight of the insights of other theories and the fact that their own necessary fictions have changed and are still changing. Their fictions become myths – ultimate and unchangeable truths about reality.

We nonetheless speak of **holding** a theory. One needs a firm base – a secure attachment, as it were – to one approach from which one can then explore others. Coming to hold a consistent orientation is rather like settling down in a relationship, after falling in and out of love and learning to live with ups and downs, disappointments and confirmations. The more one has been able to work and develop within a particular form, warts and all, the more there is of substance to integrate other approaches *into*. Hinshelwood (1985) suggests that inexperienced group therapists are unlikely to integrate the different systems of thinking when the most experienced proponents of the respective traditions have not succeeded in this themselves.

It is possible to get one's bearings in group analysis and to develop within it without undertaking a full professional training. Doing some theoretical study in a social context is a way of maintaining an open-minded and critical stance – it can also be much more fun. One way of learning with others is to form a reading group which meets regularly to discuss references followed up from the course, or articles from *Group Analysis* or to work through a classic text on the subject chapter by chapter. There are also local group-analytic cultures (see the Addresses at the end of this chapter).

The workshops put on by the Institute of Group Analysis or one of the organisations mentioned in the last three sections of this chapter take up a particular theme or concept, for instance shame, and work at it thoroughly – usually over a period of a few days. There *is* theoretical input but the main learning is by experience in small groups, interspersed with a few large group meetings. Lear (1987) noted that when we think of a colour we are bound to see it all around us. Similarly, the theme of the workshop looms so momentously large as a figure against the ground of its interpersonal network that for sometime afterwards one cannot help but construe everything one sees in terms of it, as a therapist. That is, one overdoes it. But eventually a sense of proportion is gained and what one then has is an authentic grasp of a particular aspect of human affairs – one that certainly could not have been learned as deeply from books alone.

A workshop brings together theory and practice in a way that lasts both in terms of the genuine insights gained into its particular theme and in terms of its general contribution to one's development along group-analytic lines.

A note on research

As well as theoretical development there is a need to learn in a more formal sense from the experience of conducting groups. Group therapists have often thought about research in a defensive way as having to prove the value and effectiveness of group therapy to those who have not yet been convinced (see Bednar and Kaul, 1994; Roth and Fonagy, 1996). Whitaker (1985) argues convincingly for the need to monitor and assess any groups we are conducting in order to acquire useful feedback about our efforts. In this way, as with the other tools for development, we can bring a different perspective to bear on our practice. She offers many approaches ranging from the post-session reviews, through modest clinical audit projects, to small-scale research. Her proposals for opening up practice in these ways are strongly recommended to therapists of all levels of experience. If trainees and trainers alike are to avoid the rigid certainties of the myths surrounding the theory and practice of group therapy they need such a basic 'research orientation'. Yalom (1995) refers 'not to a steel-spectacled Chi square efficiency but instead to an open, self-critical enquiring attitude toward clinical and research evidence and conclusions'. Yalom and Whitaker guard against getting carried way too much into a closed system of thinking shaped by self-evident truths concerning what group therapy is really about.

Personal therapy?

If one is about to conduct a group it is important to have been in a group oneself. It is impossible to appreciate, from books alone, the shame of disclosure, the fear of isolation and rejection, the significance of the *group,* the power it wields, how the group can make a difference for better or worse and how the conductor matters a great deal. The lack of such experience can be a major pitfall for an individual counsellor or therapist wanting to conduct a group. If one has struggled with one's own feelings and fantasies about a conductor and observed other members struggling with their own, possibly quite different, views of her, then one is less inclined to take lightly the conductor's place in the scheme of things. This is the stuff of introductory course experiential groups which teach, through personal experience, the importance of group dynamics and interpersonal relations.

Members of an *experiential* group are committing themselves to an exploration of here and now group processes, some of which may suggest signposts towards deeper, more personal and possibly thera-peutic work. Members are free to set off in the direction of therapy, but equally this is not expected of those who do *not* so wish. In a *therapy* group, the commitment is to therapeutic change as discussed in earlier chapters. In the course of therapy members obviously learn something about group dynamics along the way, and experiential groups can offer a therapeutic experience. It can seem a fine line at times, but the aims of the two types of group are clearly different.

Having learned something about what it is like to be in a group, beginning therapists may consider *personal therapy*. They may, quite appropriately, have identified a personal need for therapy which can be met in the guise of further *training*. But the actual *training* needs for therapy depend upon the developmental path one is on. It is generally accepted that one's personal therapy should be in the same modality as the therapy one practises; that is, group therapy for group therapists, individual therapy for individual therapists. However, most psychotherapeutically inclined people in the helping professions work with individuals, couples, families *and* groups. They may decide on individual personal therapy, group therapy or another experiential group, this time with the intention of following personal signposts toward therapy. The choice may also depend on local availability. If one's path leads to conducting progressively more groups at work, a personal group therapy is more appropriate. If one is conducting groups all the time the intensive analytic group experience of a full professional training is strongly recommended.

The group therapist's *equipment,* apart from a few chairs, is herself. Her effectiveness in, and enjoyment of, her work with groups will be a function of her awareness of, and ease with, herself. Personal therapy involves a private journey of exploration and it is important it occurs at the appropriate time for that individual.

Supervision

Foulkes (1975) regarded supervision as the key to the task of training the people needed for the practice of group psychotherapy in a reasonable time, given that only a few will undertake the full professional training. His approach to supervision was derived from, and consistent with, the principles of group analysis in that he worked with *groups* of supervisees learning 'in action' *about* groups *in* groups – 'including the conductor'. He emphasised the importance of clarity about the task and boundaries of the supervision group, but believed that when this was established anything *relevant* to the task could be taken up and would fall into perspective in the service of the task of supervision.

Supervision integrates many of the tools for development discussed in this chapter:

- Supervisees hear about groups other than their own: **observing groups**.
- If they are co-conductors they are supervised together. Their interaction in their therapy group will probably emerge in the supervision group too: **being a co-therapist**.
- Theory and new ideas will be discussed and familiar ones applied: **theory**.
- Supervisees deepen their understanding of themselves and of other people. Supervision may reveal aspects of the supervisee's personality which require further exploration: **personal therapy**.

This means that supervision groups are complex and both supervisor and supervisee need to think about how best to use them. Both can be seduced away from the task in hand into a preoccupation with the group setting, with the individual supervisee's blind spots or the dynamics of the supervision group itself (see Bott, 1979). The dynamics of the supervision group may have to be addressed when they are interfering with the exploration of the therapy group or when processes at work in the therapy group are being reflected in the supervision group in a way that can be usefully explored (Mattison, 1975). Similarly, supervisees can link their own personal experiences to the group material as long as they are not trying to turn the supervision into a therapy session. An article by Kadushin (1968) is a treasury of the dodges supervisors and supervisees have created in order to avoid the work of supervision.

When the supervision group is part of a course leading to a qualification the dynamics of the supervision group changes for the development of the supervisee becomes *official* business – with the supervisor to some extent in the role of assessor (actually the supervisor can feel under the scrutiny of the training body too). The supervisor may tactfully draw attention to its influence on the supervision when this occurs.

The supervisor's relationship to the real life therapy group is an odd one. Supervision has been regarded as an impossible profession since the supervisor cannot be present at the group session and so does not know what happens, yet psychologically (from the supervisee's viewpoint) she is present. It may work best if both remain aware that what they are jointly imagining is a shared fantasy rather than the truth (Zinkin, 1995).

There are also practical issues of how to facilitate several supervision group members thinking about an even larger number of group members. It is helpful to have a thumbnail sketch of the composition of each group. It may be preferable to focus on one group for several sessions until the supervision group has assimilated it. Supervisees also have to record and organise their group sessions before deciding how to present the material. Many schemes for recording are available. (Cox (1973) graphically brings a number of these concepts together.) Unless the supervisor has a particular preference, it is a good idea to experiment until you find one that suits you. Notes should include seating positions, absences (with and without apologies), lateness, a sequence of main interactions (including those on which the session opened and closed) and a summary of the main overt and covert themes.

There is then the question of *how* to present. Beginning supervisees often give exhaustive (and exhausting) details of their sessions leaving no time for discussion. Attention to what actually happened – by means of detailed notes or video or audio recordings – is important but can be at the expense of reaching beyond the minute particulars of a session through free group association, far flung metaphor and the work of imagination. The supervisor may have her own way of balancing the objective and subjective elements of supervision – which should vary according to the level of experience of the group. Sharpe and Blackwell (1987) and Sharpe (1995) illustrate several different models for presentation of group sessions to make supervisees aware of the possibility of personal choice. These include:

■ process presentation, a step-by-step account
■ brainstorming, free association around an issue
■ spontaneous report, the supervisee talks spontaneously without notes about her therapy group, memory training in action
■ following one particular patient in depth through a group
■ dramatisation or role play of a step-by-step account, with the supervisor observing
■ theoretical analysis, looking at the therapy session in terms of a particular concept such as mirroring or a single issue, such as absenteeism.

The models varied from week to week in the authors' approach to supervision, which includes the group's assessment of the supervisor.

Peer supervision can also make use of these models and be valuable particularly later on in one's development. While peer arrangements are not as challenging as groups which have someone in the role of supervisor, they are much better than nothing at all.

Organising supervision – *Supervision* means watching over the work of others with authority but the prefix *super* also means something over and above what is expected, or something in addition. The real value of supervision may be that it brings a wider range of vision than can be gained from a singular vantage point.

Many psychotherapy training organisations either provide supervision apart from their specialist trainings, or can recommend a supervisor (see later). Psychotherapy departments within the health service and relevant voluntary agencies also have supervisory resources which could provide a supervision group for group workers. We strongly recommend introductory course members to approach these services and, frankly, to pester them into responding to your request for supervision. There may be little space for thinking at work, but we owe it to ourselves, to our practice and to our patients to secure it somewhere. Pester away!

Person and Role

We have been concentrating in this chapter on the different ways in which a new group therapist can develop. For a significant minority this may mean continuing on to a commitment to full professional training. There also is increasing recognition of the need for a more graduated form of training which is currently being devised by the Institute of Group Analysis.

In the UK professional qualification as a group psychotherapist is gained after four or more years of training. This leads to registration as a psychotherapist by the United Kingdom Council for Psychotherapy (UKCP) through one's training organisation. Training in group analysis involves a personal group analysis, theoretical seminars and supervision and the writing of theoretical and clinical papers and may include an optional academic qualification. Some training takes place during the week with twice-weekly personal group analysis, others through a block-training consisting of ten weekend blocks a year with additional telephone supervision. The pros and contras of these two training models are debated elsewhere (see Behr and Hearst, 1990; Olivieri-Larsson, 1991). Courses on the block model have been established in a number of countries, enabling those who are not already in a centre for group therapy to develop professionally. All these courses build on the experience of an introductory or general course in group analysis.

Using these tools for development gives a person a widening range of actions and ideas to draw upon to enable patients to change through the active agency of the group itself. The conductor articulates her developing competence through identifying the therapeutic aim of the group and finding her special role within it. Some beginning therapists seem to grasp the role early on while others find it stuffy and alienating, mistaking the conductor's authority for authoritarianism. It is through her modest *role* in the group that the conductor can deploy her personal development in the service of the aims of therapy, and guard against using *power* to make the group perform. Hirschorn (1988) argues that we are not alienated from one another because roles separate us but that, on the contrary, we lose sight of one another when we step out of the roles which might help us collaborate. The conductor provides a new perspective to what might otherwise be a pseudo-mutual group by accepting the reality that change is difficult.

The therapist listens carefully, trying to understand, and act responsibly and empathically. She struggles to stay in role whether she is the centre of the group's attention or entirely excluded. She tries not to hide in the role or use it to dominate the group, but rather to speak through it personally and constructively. She tries not to take transference projections personally nor to dismiss genuine personal feedback as transference. These responsibilities come with the role and would be scarcely possible without the boundaries *of* the role.

It is when the reality gets too much for her, too, that she may step out of role and treat members not as they are but as she *needs* them to be, in order to alleviate her own anxiety. Genuine development as a therapist involves looking for evidence that one is getting it *wrong* using the gap between our understanding and the feedback we receive as a source of further understanding (Hobson, 1985). The research of Safran *et al.* (1990) shows that the **alliance rupture**, the breakdown in therapeutic communication jointly created by therapist and patient, is the very point at which therapy offers the greatest potential for change. This is a major training issue as it has been observed that therapists resist making a virtue out of the necessity of occasionally missing the point because of the anxiety this arouses, undermining their self-esteem. If she can get back in touch with her role, it provides the therapist with an 'observing ego' for trying to understand what her anxiety is about.

The boundaries of the group are a set of constraints to which members accommodate their day-to-day personality only to discover that the boundaries provide a space for thinking and development. The boundary of the role offers a comparable developmental space to the therapist. The role frames her creativity and learning – stepping out of role is a **boundary incident** requiring reflective thought. Theory, supervision and personal development all help her to take up the role and to continue becoming a group therapist within its boundaries. Wherever her developmental path is leading, the role requires that she follows the group in its struggles with difficulties that are not so dissimilar to her own, recognising the privileged perspective which allows her to see things differently. She can respect others, rather than using them, recognising that they share a difficult reality. Fromm-Reichmann (1949) considers such respect is a prerequisite for successful psychotherapy and stems from the conviction that one's patients' difficulties in living are not too different from one's own. Indeed Yalom (1995, pp. 204–5) quotes Foulkes as stating, 50 years ago, that the mature conductor was actually modest – her attitude towards the group would genuinely be, in Foulkes' (1945) words: 'Here we are together facing reality and the basic problems of human existence. I am one of you, not more and not less.'

Selected Organisations and their Addresses

People who have completed one of the introductory courses, or have significant experience in working analytically with groups, are eligible to apply for Associate Membership of the Group Analytic Society (London) which includes a subscription to *Group Analysis*. This rich resource reveals the inner face of group analysis and its evolving fictions.

The Group Analytic Society (London)
90 Belsize Village
Belsize Lane
London NW3 5BE

It has information about other national and international organisations including:

Group Analysis North in Manchester

Group Analysis South-West in Exeter

EGATIN (European Association for Training in Group Analysis)

Group Analysis, the Journal of the Group Analytic Society (Sage)

British Association for Group Therapy

The Institute of Group Analysis is a training organisation which accredits most of the general or introductory courses in group-analytic therapy in the UK and offers advanced group-analytic training both in the UK and internationally. Contact it for details of local courses and clinical supervision seminars. It also offers specialist group-analytic training in London, Manchester and Glasgow, leading to membership of the Institute and registration with the United Kingdom Council for Psychotherapy.

The Institute of Group Analysis
1 Daleham Gardens
London NW3 5BY

Training Organisations offering Advanced Group-analytic Training

The Institute of Group Analysis has intermediate courses at several venues which offer regular clinical supervision seminars including Bath, Brighton, Cambridge, Glasgow, London, Manchester, Sheffield, and several outside the UK.

Training Organisations offering Specialist Group-analytic Training

The Institute of Group Analysis
The Westminster Pastoral Foundation
Goldsmith's College
Sheffield University

For further information see:

UK Council for Psychotherapy
167–169 Great Portland Street
London W1N 5FB

and

British Association for Counselling

For further information about group-analytic therapy contact:

Clinical Service
The Institute of Group Analysis
1 Daleham Gardens
London NW3 5BY

BIBLIOGRAPHY

Abercrombie, M.L.J. (1989) *The Anatomy of Judgement*, London: Free Association.

Agazarian, Y. and Peters, R. (1981) *The Visible and Invisible Group*, London: Routledge.

Bacha, C. (1997) 'The stranger in the group: new members in analytic group psychotherapy', *Psychodynamic Counselling*, **3**(1): 7–23.

Balint, E. (1993) *Before I was I: Psychoanalysis and the Imagination*, London, Free Association Books.

Bednar, R. and Kaul, T.D. (1994) 'Experiential group research: Can the cannon fire?' in Bergin, A.E. and Garfield, S.L. (eds) *Handbook of Psychotherapy and Behaviour Change*, 4th edn, pp. 631–63.

Behr, H. and Hearst, L. (1990) 'Special section: block training in group analysis', *Group Analysis*, **23**(4): 339–77.

Bennis, W.G. and Shepherd, H.A. (1956) 'A theory of group development', *Human Relations*, **9**(4): 415–37.

Berger, M. (1954) 'Anxiety in groups', *American Journal of Psychotherapy*, **12**: 505–10.

Bion, W.R. (1961) *Experiences in Groups*, New York: Basic Books.

Bion, W.R. (1962) 'A theory of thinking', *International Journal of Psychoanalysis*, **43**.

Blackwell, D. (1994) 'The emergence of racism in group analysis', *Group Analysis*, **27**(2): 197–211.

Bollas, C. (1993) *Being a Character: Psychoanalysis and Self Experience*, London: Routledge.

Bott, P. (1979) 'Systems model for group psychotherapy supervision', *Group Analysis*, **12**(2): 134.

Bowlby, J. (1979) *The Making and Breaking of Affectional Bonds*, London: Tavistock.

Brown, D. and Pedder, J. (1991) *Introduction to Psychotherapy*, London: Routledge.

Cappielo, A., Zanasi, M. and Fiumara, R.S. (1988) 'The therapeutic value of the silent observer: clinical experience in group analysis', *Group Analysis*, **21**(3): 227–32.

Cox, M. (1973) 'The group therapy interaction chronogram', *British Journal of Social Work*, **3**: 243–56.

Dalal, F. (1997) 'The colour question in psychoanalysis', *Journal of Social Work Practice*, **11**(2): 103–15.

Dalal, F. (1998) *Taking the Group Seriously*, London and Philadelphia: Jessica Kingsley.

Dana, M. and Lawrence, M. (1988) *Women's Secret Disorder*, London: Grafton.

Forster, E.M. (1956) *Howard's End*, London, Edward Arnold.

Foulkes, E. (ed.) (1990) *Selected papers of S.H. Foulkes*, London: Karnac.

Foulkes, S.H. (1938) 'Book review of Norbert Elias' *The Civilising Process*' in Foulkes, E. (ed.) (1990).

Foulkes, S.H. (1945) 'A memorandum on group therapy', British Military Memorandum ADM in Yalom, I. (1995), pp. 204–5.

Foulkes, S.H. (1948) *Introduction to Group-Analytic Psychotherapy*, London: Maresfield Reprints.

Foulkes, S.H. (1964) *Therapeutic Group Analysis*, London: George Allen & Unwin.

Foulkes, S.H. (1972) 'Oedipus conflict and regression' in Foulkes, E. (ed.) (1990).

Foulkes, S.H. (1975) *Group Analytic Psychotherapy*, London: Gordon and Breach.

Foulkes, S.H. and Anthony, E.J. (1957) *Group Psychotherapy: The Psychoanalytic Approach*, Harmondsworth: Penguin.

Frank, J.D. and Frank, J.B. (1991) *Persuasion and Healing: A Comparative Study of Psychotherapy*, 3rd edn, Baltimore: Johns Hopkins University Press.

Freud, S. (1974) *Introductory Lectures on Psychoanalysis*, Harmondsworth: Penguin.

Fromm-Reichmann, F. (1949) 'Notes on personal and professional requirements of a psychotherapist' in Bullard, D.M. (ed.) *Psychoanalysis and Psychotherapy: Selected Papers*, Chicago: University of Chicago Press.

Garland, C. (1982) 'Group-analysis: Taking the non-problem seriously', *Group Analysis*, **15**(1): 4–14.

Garland, C. (1991) 'External disasters and the internal world: an approach to understanding survivors', in Holmes, J. (ed.) *Textbook of Psychotherapy in Psychiatric Practice*, Edinburgh: Churchill Livingstone.

Grotjahn, M. (1983) 'The qualities of the group psychotherapist' in Kaplan, H. and Sadock, B. (eds) *Comprehensive Group Psychotherapy*, Baltimore: Williams and Wilkins.

Gustafson, J.P. (1976) 'The pseudo-mutual small group or institution', *Human Relations*, **29**: 989–97.

Harwood, I. and Pines, M. (eds) (1998) *Self Experiences in Group*, London and Philadelphia: Jessica Kingsley.

Hinshelwood, R.D. (1985) 'The patient's defensive analyst', *British Journal of Psychotherapy*, **2**(1): 30–41.

Hirschorn, L. (1998) *The Workplace Within: Psychodynamics of Organisational Life*, Cambridge, MA: MIT Press.

Hobbs, M. (1988) 'From behind the scenes: the psychodynamic implications for an analytic group of being observed through a one-way screen', *Group Analysis*, **21**(3): 235–48.

Hobson, R.F. (1985) *Forms of Feelings: The Heart of Psychotherapy*, London: Tavistock.

Hoggett, P. (1992) *Partisans in an Uncertain World: The Psychoanalysis of Engagement*, London: Free Association Books.

Home, H.J. (1983) 'The effect of numbers on the basic transference pattern in group analysis', in Pines, M. (1983).

Hudson, I. (1990) 'Heterogeneity and homogeneity in groups', unpublished paper.

Hyde, K. (1991) 'Idealisation and omnipotence within the group matrix', *Group Analysis*, **24**(3): 279–89.

Jacques, E. (1955) 'Social systems as a defence against persecutory and depressive anxiety', in Klein, M., Heimann, P. and Money-Kyrle, R.E. (eds) *New Directions in Psychoanalysis*, New York: Basic Books, pp. 478–98.

James, D.C. (1994) 'Holding and containing in the group and society', in Brown, D. and Zinkin, L. (eds) *The Psyche and the Social World*, London: Routledge.

Kadushin, A. (1968) 'Games people play in supervision', *Social Work*, **13**(3): 23–32.

Kauff, P.F. (1977) 'The termination process: its relation to the separation–individuation phase of development', *International Journal of Group Psychotherapy*, **27**: 3–18.

Kennard, D., Roberts, J. and Winter, D.A. (1993) *A Work Book of Group Analytic Interventions*, London: Routledge.

Kohut, H. (1984) *How Does Analysis Cure?*, London: University of Chicago Press.

Lear, T. (1987) 'Studies of shame', *Group Analysis*, **20**(1): 15.

Lear, T. (1988) 'Therapeutic value of the silent observer. Discussion on paper by Cappiello, A., Zanasi, M. and Fiumara, R.S.', *Group Analysis*, **22**(3): 232.

Lewin, K. (1951) *Field Theory in Social Science*, New York: Harper & Row.

Maar, V. (1989) 'Attempts at grasping the self during the termination phase of group-analytic psychotherapy', *Group Analysis*, **22**(1): 99–104.

Malan, D. (1979) *Individual Psychotherapy and the Science of Psychodynamics*, London: Butterworth.

Mann, D. (1989) 'Incest: the father and the male therapist', *British Journal of Psychotherapy*, **6**(2): 143–53.

Marrone, M. and Diamond, N. (1998) *Attachment and Interaction*, London and Philadelphia: Jessica Kingsley.

Mattinson, J. (1975) *The Reflection Process in Casework Supervision*, London: Institute of Marital Studies.

Menzies-Lyth, I. (1959) 'The functioning of social systems as a defence against anxiety', reprinted in *Containing Anxiety in Institutions: Selected Essays*, London: Free Association Books, 1988, pp. 43–85.

Miller, L., Rustin, M. and Shuttleworth, J. (eds) (1989) *Closely Observed Infants*, London: Duckworth.

Mollon, P. (1989) 'Anxiety, supervision and a space for thinking: some narcissistic perils for clinical psychologists in learning psychotherapy', *British Journal of Medical Psychology*, **62**: 113–22.

Morgan, G. (1986) *Images of Organisation,* London: Sage.

Mullan, H. and Rosenbaum, M. (1978) *Group Psychotherapy: Theory and Practice*, New York: Free Press.

Nitsun, M. (1989) 'Early development: linking the individual and the group', *Group Analysis*, **22**(3): 249–61.

Obholzer, A. (1994) 'Managing social anxieties in public sector organizations', in Obholzer, A. and Zagier Roberts, V. (eds) *The Unconscious at Work*, London: Routledge, pp. 169–79.

Okun, B. (1997) *Effective Helping: Interviewing and Counselling Techniques*, 5th edn, Pacific Grove, CA: Brooks/Cole.

Olivieri-Larsson, R. (1991) 'Block training in group analysis: comment on special section', *Group Analysis*, **24**(3): 335.

Parry Crooke, G. (1980) *A Study of Self-Help Groups for Compulsive Eaters*, London: Health Education Council.

Pines, M. (1979) Therapeutic factors in group analytic psychotherapy, personal communication.

Pines, M. (1983) *The Evolution of Group Analysis*, London: Routledge.

Pines, M. (1985) 'Psychic development and the group analytic situation', *Group*, **9**(1): 24–37.

Pines, M. (1993) 'Interpretation why, for whom and when?', in Kennard, D., Roberts, J. and Winter, D.A. (eds) *A Workbook of Group-Analytic Interventions*, pp. 98–103.

Pines, M. (1998) *Circular Reflections*, London and Philadelphia: Jessica Kingsley.

Pines, M., Hearst, L.E. and Behr, H.L. (1982) 'Group analysis (Group analytic psychotherapy)' in Gazda, G.M. (ed.) *Basic Approaches to Group Psychotherapy and Group Counselling*, 3rd edn, Springfield, IL: Charles Thomas.

Redl, F. (1966) 'What is there to *see* about a group?' in Redl, F. *When We Deal with Children: Selected Writings*, New York: Free Press.

Rippa, B. (1994) 'Groups in Israel during the Gulf War', *Group Analysis*, **27**(1): 87–94.

Rohr, E. (1993) 'In the church; ethnopsychoanalytic research in Ecuador', *Group Analysis*, **26**(3): 295–306.

Rosenfeld, A. and Dawson, A.C. (1993) 'A first experience of running a group for sexually abused women in an acute psychiatric setting', *Journal of Social Work Practice*, **7**(2): 163–71.

Roth, A. and Fonagy, P. (1996) *What Works for Whom? A Critical Review of Psychotherapy Research*, New York: Guilford Press.

Rothenberg, A. (1988) *The Creative Process of Psychotherapy*, New York: W.W. Norton.

Safran, J.D. *et al.* (1990) 'Therapeutic alliance rupture as a therapy event for empirical investigation', *Psychotherapy*, **27**(2): 154–65.

Samuels, A. (1964) 'Use of group balance as a therapeutic technique', *Archives of General Psychiatry*, **11**: 411.

Schafer, R. (1983) *The Analytic Attitude*, London: Hogarth Press.

Schein, E.H. (1987) *Process Consultation*, Reading, MA: Addison-Wesley.

Schindler, W. (1966) 'The role of the mother in group psychotherapy', *International Journal of Group Psychotherapy*, **16**: 198–202.

Sharpe, M. (1995) *The Third Eye*, London: Routledge.

Sharpe, M. and Blackwell, D. (1987) 'Creative supervision through student involvement', *Group Analysis*, **20**(3): 195–208.

Skovholt, T. and Ronnestad, M.H. (1992) *The Evolving Professional Staff: Stages and Themes in Therapist and Counsellor Development*, Chichester: John Wiley.

Skynner, A.C.R. (1989) *Institutes and How to Survive Them*, London: Methuen.

Terry, P. (1997) *Counselling the Elderly and their Carers*, London: Macmillan.

Tuckman, B. (1965) 'Developmental sequences in small groups', *Psychological Bulletin*, **63**: 384–99.

Turquet, P. (1975) 'Threats to identity in the large group', in Kreeger, L. (ed.) *The Large Group*, London: Maresfield Reprints, pp. 87–145.

Wardi, D. (1989) 'The termination phase in the group process', *Group Analysis*, **22**(1): 87–99.

Whitaker, D.S. (1985) *Using Groups to Help People*, London: Routledge & Kegan Paul.

Whitaker, D.S. (1992) 'Transposing learnings from group psychotherapy to work groups', *Group Analysis*, **25**(2): 131–49.

Whitaker, D.S. and Lieberman, M.A. (1964) *Psychotherapy through the Group Process*, New York and London: Prentice-Hall.

Williams, M. (1966) 'Limitations, fantasies and security: operations of beginning group therapists', *International Journal of Group Psychotherapy*, **16**(1): 150–62.

Winnicott, D.W. (1960) 'The theory of the parent–infant relationship', in Winnicott, D.W. *The Maturational Processes and the Facilitating Environment*, London: Hogarth, 1965.

Winnicott, D.W. (1964) *The Child, the Family and the Outside World*, Harmondsworth: Penguin.

Winnicott, D.W. (1971) *Playing and Reality*, Harmondsworth: Peguin.

Winnicott, D.W. (1982) *Through Paediatrics to Psychoanalysis*, London: Hogarth Press.

Woodhouse, D. and Pengelly, P. (1991) *Anxiety and the Dynamics of Collaboration*, Aberdeen: Aberdeen University Press.

Yalom, I. (1975) *The Theory and Practice of Group Psychotherapy*, 2nd edn, New York: Basic Books.

Yalom, I. (1995) *The Theory and Practice of Group Psychotherapy*, 4th edn, New York: Basic Books.

Zinkin, L. (1995) 'Supervision: the impossible profession', in Kugler, P. (ed.) *Jungian Perspectives on Supervision*, Switzerland: Daimon Verlag.

INDEX